The Art of Cyber Security

A practical guide to winning the war on
cyber crime

The Art of Cyber Security

A practical guide to winning the war on cyber crime

GARY HIBBERD

IT Governance Publishing

Every possible effort has been made to ensure that the information contained in this book is accurate at the time of going to press, and the publisher and the author cannot accept responsibility for any errors or omissions, however caused. Any opinions expressed in this book are those of the author, not the publisher. Websites identified are for reference only, not endorsement, and any website visits are at the reader's own risk. No responsibility for loss or damage occasioned to any person acting, or refraining from action, as a result of the material in this publication can be accepted by the publisher or the author.

Apart from any fair dealing for the purposes of research or private study, or criticism or review, as permitted under the Copyright, Designs and Patents Act 1988, this publication may only be reproduced, stored or transmitted, in any form, or by any means, with the prior permission in writing of the publisher or, in the case of reprographic reproduction, in accordance with the terms of licences issued by the Copyright Licensing Agency. Enquiries concerning reproduction outside those terms should be sent to the publisher at the following address:

IT Governance Publishing Ltd
Unit 3, Clive Court
Bartholomew's Walk
Cambridgeshire Business Park
Ely, Cambridgeshire
CB7 4EA
United Kingdom
www.itgovernancepublishing.co.uk

The author has asserted the rights of the author under the Copyright, Designs and Patents Act, 1988, to be identified as the author of this work.

Paperback first published in the United Kingdom in 2022 by IT Governance Publishing.
ISBN 978-1-78778-365-2 (pb.)

Hardback first published in 2024 by IT Governance Publishing.
ISBN 978-1-78778-557-1 (hc.)

ABOUT THE AUTHOR

As many books do, I should start by telling you about my business background to build some credibility. I should tell you about my 40 years in cyber security and how I have worked for many multinational organisations like GE Money, and others.

If you're interested in that, please check out my LinkedIn page:

www.linkedin.com/in/garyhibberd/.

But I'd rather start this book in a slightly different way.

Let me take you back to where my love of all things tech-related began.

At the age of nine, I saw the movie *Star Wars: A New Hope*, which dramatically impacted my young life. I quickly became obsessed with the film, and amassed all the information and toys I could relating to the franchise. But the obsession didn't end with collecting the latest duvet cover emblazoned with Luke Skywalker and Darth Vader. I also wanted to understand the mythology of the Jedi and the Sith. In my quest for knowledge, I discovered that George Lucas, the creator of *Star Wars*, took a lot of inspiration from the samurai and the samurai's approach to life and death. From that moment, I was hooked and wanted to learn all I could about Japanese culture and the samurai. Ultimately, this led me to learn about the ninja, and the martial art Bujinkan Taijutsu, which mixes physical training with history and philosophy.

In that training, I discovered how samurai lived and how they prepared for battle. When learning about military leaders, particularly East Asian leaders, it is impossible not to come across the work of Sun Tzu. This military strategist is at the core of this book, and we will return to him shortly.

At the age of 28, I achieved the much-coveted black belt, but as anyone who trains in martial arts will tell you, this is just the start of your journey. After all, anyone can 'own' a black belt, but few 'are' a black belt.

Although I have studied martial arts for the better part of 40 years, my professional passion has always been computers and technology. Again, another movie I saw sparked a passion that has never diminished: *WarGames*. This 1983 film tells the story of a young hacker who almost starts World War III when he hacks into a military base and plays a 'war game', which turns out to be more accurate than he imagined! My interest was piqued, and I wanted to understand this new world of computers and networks that was emerging. So that's what I did. I have been fortunate to work for global banks, retail, and the public and private sectors, helping them achieve higher degrees of security and data protection. I have helped shape the industry by assisting in the development of international standards like ISO 27001 (information security management) and ISO 22301 (business continuity management), and writing books or chapters for books that are educating the next generation of cyber professionals.

Fast forward to today, and I've been a cyber security consultant and data protection specialist for more than 35 years, helping companies and individuals put security controls in place that protect them and their businesses. Every day, our world changes, and security has moved from being very operational to ever more strategic and tactical. I have increasingly seen the connection between cyber security and martial arts, and my approach to the protection of companies, data and individuals has been shaped by the martial arts I have studied.

So that's me: a martial artist who is passionate about cyber security and data protection. Now you know me a little better, let's get on with this!

ACKNOWLEDGEMENTS

I am constantly inspired by the myriad of cyber security professionals I have come across in my professional life, and I would therefore like to acknowledge their contribution here. I have learned a great deal from many of them, and I count myself fortunate to have such inspirational cyber security professionals in my circle of friends. The insights and experiences I recount in this book are drawn from my time spent with them, so I would like to thank them and to dedicate this book to them.

This book would also not have happened without the love and support of my family. My wife Sue has believed in me and given gentle encouragement throughout the writing process. Her patience and understanding of all that I do has been instrumental in helping me achieve career highs and survive career lows. I am thankful to my incredible children Luke and Jessica, who keep me honest and hold me to account for my words and deeds. I'd also like to dedicate this book to the memory of Maureen Drake, a wonderful woman who demonstrated what love and commitment are on a daily basis.

I would like to make a special mention of my friend and colleague Lee Scorey, who was there for me when it mattered most. I will be forever grateful for his friendship, professionalism and pragmatism and for encouraging me when times were hardest.

I would like to thank Yinka Akingbehin, Chris Evans, Marc van Delft and Christopher Wright for their helpful comments during the production of this book. I would also like to thank

Acknowledgements

Nicola Day, publications manager at IT Governance Publishing.

Finally, this book is dedicated to you, dear reader. People like you are daring to look at cyber security differently, and therefore will ultimately make a difference in the world. I hope you will use the ideas and principles in this book to expand your thinking on the topics of cyber security, information security and data protection. I wish you well in this endeavour, and I hope you keep this book to hand as a source of inspiration when needed most.

FOREWORD

The problem with writing is that it's so difficult to know where to start. It's hard to decide what your important first words should be. For this foreword, I'll begin by stealing (er... 'borrowing') some of Gary's words from this very book:

"Cyber criminals know where our attention is, and they are masters of deception and misdirection, attacking us when we are looking the other way. They are using every trick in the book to exploit our one-dimensional thinking. The solution? We need to improve our thinking."

AND

"Anyone can get into cyber security, just like anyone can draw. But the truly great cyber security people out there are artists. They use their hands, heads and hearts to create something special."

That's what this book is about. If you're here looking for reference architectures or step-by-step "how to be a CISO" guides, then you are in the wrong place. THIS is a book about building the mindset and approach needed to survive cyber battles, lead your army, match wits with your enemies, and successfully plan for war. The journey to acquiring that mindset begins simply enough: know thyself.

I think that's one of the main things I appreciate so much about Gary's approach to cyber security and risk management. Gary understands that cyber security is a game of understanding strengths and weaknesses while also trying to manage unknowns. That means understanding our strengths and weaknesses, and our many enemies' potential strengths and weaknesses, and accounting (as much as we can) for unknowns. This type of awareness can be challenging to achieve – but pays off in preparedness, strength and resilience.

There are two other aspects of Gary's work that I have a sincere appreciation for. First, Gary takes a meta approach to cyber security. He begins by seeking the abstraction so as to find first principles: those fundamental truths or assumptions that cannot be deduced from any other propositions or assumptions. Then, he seeks to demonstrate how the principle applies to the specific problems we face. This is the fundamental key to helping build a mindset that will grow and flex over time, adapting (rather than snapping) as new trends and technologies emerge. I always picture this ability to adapt and flow with change as being similar to Neo at the end of the original *Matrix* movie, ducking and weaving around the onslaught of bullets hurtling his way.

The other aspect of Gary's approach that I appreciate is his continued focus on the human element. Gary knows that just because we throw the word 'cyber' about all the time doesn't mean that all of our problems and approaches to mitigating the threats involve technology. The truth is often the opposite: the mitigation critically involves understanding and accounting for humans.

And, speaking of humans, Gary is one of the good ones. I also believe that you, dear reader, are too. You decided to pick up this book at this specific time and are now reading these particular words. Something drew you to the title and topic. And now it's time to dive in. Let's get ready to know ourselves, know our enemy and learn the art of cyber security.

Perry Carpenter

Chief evangelist and strategy officer for KnowBe4, author and podcaster

PREFACE

> *"To romanticize the world is to make us aware of the magic, mystery and wonder of the world; it is to educate the senses to see the ordinary as extraordinary, the familiar as strange, the mundane as sacred, the finite as infinite."*
>
> Novalis
>
> (poet, author and philosopher of Early German Romanticism)

DO NOT SKIP THIS SECTION!

I'm going to get straight to the point: some of you will not like this book.

Not. One. Little. Bit.

Why? Because it isn't your typical cyber security book. It's going to challenge you. It's going to make you stop and think. If it doesn't, then you're going to need to reread it. This book only contains around 40,000 words and 150 pages and could easily be read in a day or two. But if you do, you've missed the point.

Take your time with the book. Once you've finished, work your way through the 'Required Reading' section at the end. Note that it is not *further* reading, because that would suggest the books are merely recommended. They are more than that. I see them as essential reading, as they build on the ideas I'm introducing here.

You may have noticed that the front cover of this book has an image of a lock with a chain and heavy padlock. But you would be wrong if you thought I selected this image because the book is about cyber security. This book is indeed about cyber security, but it's also so much more. It's about giving you the key to your creativity. It is about releasing you from the chains that hold you down and hold you back from thinking creatively and creating something amazing. No, it's not a self-help book, but it will help you be yourself and help make the world a safer place. I'm a hopeless business romantic, which is a term coined by marketing consultant and author Tim Leberecht. Like him, I am passionate about business and believe we all have the ability to love what we do.

The aim of this book is to do just that – help you fall in love with what you do and look at our industry and yourself with new eyes.

To do this, I've broken this book into two sections; both deserve equal consideration and time. The first section discusses my thoughts about our industry and those that operate within it. I believe we are all artists, and this section explains in detail why I believe this and why I want you to believe it too.

The second section is dedicated to Sun Tzu and his influential military treatise, *The Art of War*.[1] Examining and expanding upon his words through the lens of cyber security and data protection, I would like you to consider how you can apply his thinking to your profession.

At this point, you may be wondering why there are two topics covered in one book; well, the answer is relatively simple.

---

[1] Throughout this book, the quotations from *The Art of War* have been sourced from the following edition: *The Art of War* (2010), Capstone Publishing, UK: Padstow.

This book started as a series of thoughts about what we do and how we do it. Over the years, I built upon these thoughts, drawing on my experiences in martial arts, at management conferences and companies I worked for, and with the cyber security sector in general. This book is the culmination of that, putting my musings in order and outlining an approach I think we should all take. I hope you can find meaning in these pages and apply it to your world, too.

Why I wrote this book: because we need it

In 2019, the UK Active Defence report stated that UK residents are more likely to be victims of cyber crime and fraud than any other crime.[2]

In 2020, BT asked more than 7,000 business leaders, employees and consumers globally about their opinions on cyber security, with some interesting results. First, it highlighted considerable confidence that suitable security measures are in place, as 76% of business leaders rated their organisation as 'excellent' or 'good' for protecting against cyber threats. However, the same report revealed that eight out of ten executives stated their employer had suffered a security incident in the past two years.[3]

For many years, it seemed as though only heavily regulated industries were interested in data protection and cyber security. From financial services to health, education and public utilities, they prioritised cyber security because their regulators compelled them. However, following a series of dramatic, headline-grabbing cyber attacks, such as

---

[2] *www.ncsc.gov.uk/report/acd-report-year-three*.
[3] *https://newsroom.bt.com/new-research-finds-that-the-expectations-of-chief-information-security-officers-have-never-been-greater/*.

WannaCry in 2017, many more organisations began to realise that they too could fall victim. And then 2020 happened.

The COVID-19 pandemic has further increased the risks we face, as we saw cyber criminals capitalise on the fear, uncertainty and doubt (FUD) that gripped the world. In Q2 2020, Action Fraud in the UK reported a 400% increase in reported phishing attacks, with scammers using the pandemic as a source of revenue.[4] Note that this is only *reported* phishing attacks. What about all the unreported attacks? Did you report the last phishing email that landed in your inbox? Probably not. A police officer once said to me that when a crime is reported, you should multiply the number by ten to get a more accurate picture of the crime level. Of course, this is not scientific, and we can never be sure, but we could be looking at an increase of 6,500% in phishing attacks. I'm not suggesting that we should run to the police every time we receive a phishing email, but I am saying it should be reported to someone! A phishing email is a symptom and could be an indication that something isn't quite working to filter out attempts to break into your systems. I often say to people, if you were walking down the street and someone jumped out at you every day and asked you for your wallet and your PIN code, would you report it? The answer is always yes! This is what is happening in our virtual world, yet people aren't reporting it.

So why is the reporting of cyber attacks so low? Why don't people raise the flag when they've suffered an attack? There are several reasons for this, and cyber criminals are aware of

---

[4] *www.actionfraud.police.uk/alert/coronavirus-related-fraud-reports-increase-by-400-in-march*.

them all. Let's focus on phishing emails for a second; when someone clicks a malicious link and is subject to a phishing attack, their response will depend on what happens next. They might not even notice anything has happened. For example, keylogger malware downloaded from an infected email will sit quietly in the background collecting information, and the victim will be unaware until days, weeks or months later when they are alerted to some fraud. If the payload is ransomware and the victim's device or information is made inaccessible, the first thing the user will do is call their IT support person – whether that's their child, partner, friend or IT department. Next on the list is likely to be the bank to inform them that their accounts might be compromised. If the phishing email contains malware or ransomware, the victim might even call the police. But what about corporations that fall victim? Why aren't they calling the police or Action Fraud? Yes, some will inform the police as they may have insurance policies requiring a police case number, but the response is often internally focused. Why? To put it simply: brand protection.

If a cyber attack hits an organisation, the reality is that there will be a heavy focus on brand protection and damage limitation. It may sound cynical, and there are exceptions to every rule, but when a CEO or business owner tells you *after* a breach that security and data protection are their number one priority, they are not telling you the whole truth. We've seen this countless times over the decades, where a breach has impacted organisations and customers only hear about it months later, after the company had "completed internal investigations". If security and data protection were truly the number one priority, the business would have informed customers at the earliest opportunity, when it discovered the breach, so they weren't left at risk from cyber criminals. But they often don't, preferring instead to conduct internal investigations to find someone to blame, speak to their lawyers or insurers, create a positive marketing campaign to drown out any negative press, and perhaps sell shares in their company before the news breaks.

Cyber criminals know all of this and capitalise on it.

Why I wrote this book: because I needed to

As I said above, this book grew from thoughts I had over many years, It began when I first started studying martial arts, which was around the same time I started down this technological path, in the early 1980s. I saw a lot of parallels between the cyber security professionals, martial arts and artists that I worked with and trained with. Anyone who studies martial arts for any length of time will most certainly come across the military strategist Sun Tzu, who is credited for writing a series of documents that became *The Art of War*, or more accurately 'The Art of Strategy'. Although his words on military strategy, tactics and operations were written more than 2,000 years ago, I am often struck with how relevant his words are today.

The longer I work in the cyber security sector, the more I am convinced that every cyber criminal must at some point have read Sun Tzu and is using his teachings against us. This is an important point that I do not want you to miss. As you read the pages dedicated to Sun Tzu, I want you to place yourself in the mind of both business leaders and a cyber criminal. You'll quickly see that ignoring the words of Sun Tzu could leave you at greater risk of attack.

These thoughts have occupied my mind and shaped my career for the longest time, and the more I thought, the more I knew I needed to write them down. I started writing this book because I wanted somewhere I could collect my ideas on a topic I have been passionate about all my life. It started out as a series of short blogs, notes, and opinions on security and privacy, but each section grew a little longer and more reflective as I wrote. Although I love what I do, there have been times when I forgot how important and impactful our roles are. I also found it challenging to find new ways to learn, inspire or think about our discipline so that we think about it differently. It's essential to do this to keep our interest and passions in the job high, because if we're not, how can we expect anyone else to be?

So the notes I wrote became pages, and those pages became this book. In writing it, I want to reignite a flame in you for these topics, which may have dimmed over the years or even gone out altogether. It happens to the best of us, me included.

I wrote this book to challenge your thinking on key topics and force you to approach cyber security and data protection from theoretical, philosophical, strategic, tactical and operational perspectives. But I also wrote this book as a 'love letter' to the industry and to all those who serve within it. Although there are countless books about cyber security and data protection, there are very few (if any) about you and me, the professionals. I believe those who are successful in this field are tenacious, passionate, knowledgeable, dedicated, caring and hard-working but frequently undervalued, unappreciated and misunderstood. The first part of this book is dedicated to each of us who have felt this way. It is a reminder of how astounding our profession is, how significant our roles are, and our individual contribution's brilliance. I want to inspire and encourage you when you feel like all is lost or when you're feeling undervalued and unappreciated. It's a section that I wish someone had given to me when I felt this way.

I wrote this book for you, my weary fellow-traveller on the cyber super-highway. Our task is often a thankless one, and I wanted to write something that would motivate you to continue, even when the road seems long and arduous. Our roles are not easy. But if it were easy, everyone would be doing it, and what we do is pretty cool, right? I have huge admiration for anyone who puts their heart and soul into what they do, irrespective of their profession. Whether you're an accountant and you get 'giddy' at the thought of balancing the books or a road sweeper whose heart swells with joy when you see the roads you've cleaned, you have my unwavering admiration. I firmly believe the best consultants, compliance officers, engineers, analysts, designers, developers and strategists are those who put their mind, body and soul into what they do. They are true artists and can create great things. Unfortunately, as we all know, art and artists often go unnoticed or undervalued.

Finally, I wrote this book to help all of us when times are most challenging, and we need someone to remind us that what we do has merit. I wrote this book to remind you just how vital your role is. We are often underappreciated when everything is going well but quickly vilified and blamed when someone makes a mistake or an attack occurs. There is still a sense of despair and frustration within our industry that we are often seen as 'scapegoats' when it all goes wrong.

I genuinely believe what we do matters. 'Data' is so prevalent, and technology is so intrinsically important to our lives that protecting data and people who use technology is incredibly important. From children to adults, from individuals to corporations, professionals working to protect them have a tough job. We need this book to inspire us and keep us strong when things become a little less certain. We need this book to remind ourselves that nothing around us is guaranteed and that other people and other professionals don't get it right every time, either. There are no certainties.

I wrote this book to encourage us to look at our approach in a new way and give a broader context to the world in which we operate, which I know is needed.

There are countless books out there that tell us how we should be protecting ourselves and our organisations, and some discuss at great length the risks and dangers we all face. I can, have and will add to that body of work, but for now, I wanted to write something that would stir the reader into action and encourage you to think differently and ignite your imagination. I wanted to write something that would challenge you to think about these topics in a different way. Why? Because I think this topic deserves this level of contemplation. What we do is too important to be sidelined or ignored.

In the modern world, cyber security and data protection professionals need a new kind of book. To win the hearts and minds of those we seek to serve, we need to speak from the head AND the heart. I wrote this book to do just that. It is for people who see the world for what it can be, not for what it is. It is for you, me and a world that desperately needs us to be there for them. This book may polarise people: some will get it, others won't. Either way, I'll be happy because it creates a discussion about a new way of thinking.

We need to look at cyber security and data protection differently, from a fresh perspective, if we are going to win this war against cyber crime. I believe we're currently losing. The previous section outlined the reasons for this; we're living in an ever-expanding technological era that is growing ever more complex. It's becoming too complicated for one person to understand, yet we're expected to have all the answers. Like some 'all-seeing and all knowing' Wizard of Oz, we hide behind the curtain, pulling levers and pushing buttons that keep everyone safe, often receiving no recognition for our efforts.

We need this book to give us a different perspective on these topics and hopefully inspire us to think differently about our industry and our place within it.

Finally, I want this book to inspire you and remind you that we're in this together, we're stronger together, and there is always a new way of looking at our industry and the world around us. I want to show you that it's possible for each of us to change the world. It will not tell you how to do this. That's for you to find out.

If this book does nothing other than this, then it has served its purpose.

Also, I wanted to let you know that you are doing amazing and important work. On behalf of the world; thank you.

Unless stated otherwise, all quotes that are cited as Sun Tzu are sourced from The Art of War (2010), Capstone Publishing.

CONTENTS

Contents

Part 1: The mindset of an artist

" Every child is an artist.

The problem is how to remain an artist
once we grow up. "

Pablo Picasso

CHAPTER 1: INTRODUCTION

> *"If you're willing to do something that might not work, you're closer to being an artist."*
>
> Seth Godin

To be successful in cyber security takes tenacity, skill, knowledge and experience, but it takes much more to be really good at it. I firmly believe every person who dedicates their life to cyber security and data protection is an artist or has the potential to be. Some are great, and some are not so great, but we are still artists.

Many of us are overworked, overwhelmed and overlooked, and that is the world of an artist and a cyber security professional. Cyber security is fluid, ever-evolving and constantly changing, and we need to change and adapt to it. We are increasingly frustrated by the people we look to help and their inability to understand the enormity of the task we have before us. We are the ones tasked with the protection of 'data', an ethereal thing that few people (outside of our industry) genuinely understand, yet every one of us is creating more and more of it! At the time of writing, it is estimated that more than half of the globe are Internet users, with an estimated 5 billion users on a planet with 7.5 billion people.[5] All these people are creating, sharing and consuming ever-increasing amounts of data, and we are expected to keep it and them safe.

We often refer to data as information or use the terms interchangeably. But in truth, you can't have information

---

[5] *https://datareportal.com/global-digital-overview*.

(aka "content") without data. It all starts with these 'bits and byte' and builds from there. 'Data' is the plural of the Latin 'datum', meaning 'thing', so in reality, it is a loose concept that can mean everything or nothing at all. Data can be innocuous and may mean nothing to anyone, but when loose bits of data are pulled together, it leads to intelligence, it leads to information that can be used for any purpose the person holding that information chooses. This use of large quantities of data has now become an industry and focus all of its own, as we see the emergence and dominance of the 'big data' industry. The idea of big data has been around since 2005 and refers to large data sets that are almost impossible to manage and process using traditional business intelligence tools.

Data ultimately gives us answers to difficult questions, and the more data available, the more questions we can answer. Data, therefore, gives us information about the world around us, which can help inform our decisions. This process is popularly represented as the 'DIKW pyramid' which has been around in various forms since 1955. DIKW stands for;

- **Data**;
- **Information**;
- **Knowledge**; and
- **Wisdom**.

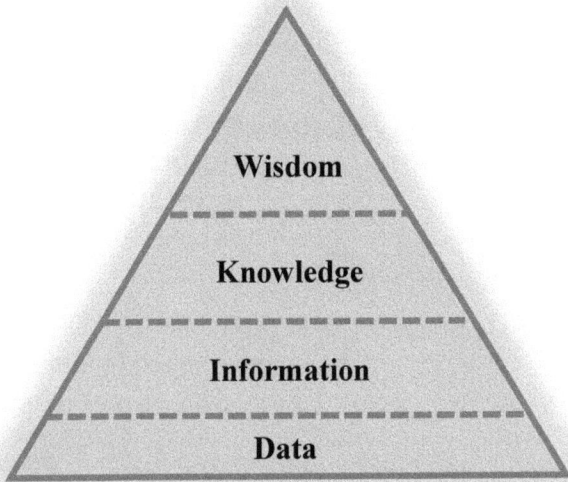

Figure 1: The DIKW Pyramid

But it is only now that we are seeing the real impact of data leading to wisdom.

This journey from data to wisdom is one that every marketing executive knows and understands, and it's the model that organisations like Amazon and Facebook are built upon.

Organisations can take fragments of 'data points' that give them information on how individuals interact and how sections of society will respond to a particular stimulus. The world of big data provides insight into how society operates, thinks and behaves. It tells us how relationships work in the 21st century, how they are formed and broken, and how each one of us can be influenced and manipulated to behave in specific ways. This knowledge can help organisations make strategic (wise) decisions about their products and how they are presented to us. Big data gives organisations the 'edge' they need when approaching and influencing our decisions.

There is a whole body of work dedicated to explaining the steps taken from data through to wisdom. But by simply being aware of this relationship between data and wisdom, it should hopefully become apparent why so many organisations greedily absorb and collect data and why it is so important that we protect it.

Data is everywhere, so data protection is vitally important. Data protection cannot be bought, bolted on or blagged, and as information is derived from data, it makes information security equally important.

In 2022, there are approximately 11.57 billion devices connected wirelessly to the internet, and this is expected to grow to 25.44 billion by 2030.[6] Everything from mobile phones and game consoles to refrigerators and home CCTV can be remotely controlled over the Internet. We certainly are living in interesting times, as we move from the 'Internet of Things' (IoT) to the 'Internet of Everything' (IoE); from science fiction to science fact, we are living in a world where everything, including people, is becoming part of this global network of 'things'. We have quickly moved from 'wearable' devices to having devices inserted into our bodies. Pacemakers, for example, are now 'Bluetooth enabled', able to monitor the efficiency of the heart and alert the emergency services to any potential problems. We are increasingly using systems and applications that rely upon machine learning, artificial intelligence (AI) and Cloud

---

[6] *www.statista.com/statistics/1183457/iot-connected-devices-worldwide/*.

computing to the point that many people don't even realise that these technologies are being used.

There is no doubt that our reliance on technology will only increase, as the flexibility and power they bring are further utilised and advanced, always with society's betterment in mind. We shouldn't forget that technology offers us tremendous opportunities. However, it also presents us with life-altering and potentially life-threatening threats – risk is a double-edged sword, with 'threat' and 'opportunity' on opposite sides.

Technology and the digital world we inhabit should not be feared; it must be understood. I'm not saying you need to understand how all this technology works, but we must try to understand how it affects each of us, both individually and collectively. Undoubtedly, we have reaped incredible benefits from this technology, but what is the trade-off for using these systems and devices? Yes, they make our lives easier, but in our rush to use more and more technology, who is thinking about how these things are being designed and built? Where is their development, design and deployment strategy? What is the focus for those creating these systems and services? Is the protection of our data at the top of their agenda? Or is functionality and data collection more important? If we do not stop to think about these questions, we are leaving ourselves at risk of exploitation, extortion and mishap from those that would seek to do us ill. Cyber criminals everywhere know how eager we are to adopt these new technologies, and they watch us from the shadows as we struggle with it too.

For this reason, I believe an arms race is taking place between cyber criminals and the rest of society. Unfortunately, I think cyber criminals are winning. There are several reasons for this. Perhaps the most obvious is that criminals don't play by the same rules as the rest of us. Consider for a moment how they conduct their business.

Cyber criminals don't care about things like health and safety laws or jurisdiction or international data protection laws. They may be interested because they use that information against us, but criminals are happy to employ underage hackers or people working long and arduous hours in horrible conditions, or build tools that can be 'tested' on the unsuspecting public. For example, when a business wishes to begin marketing to customers, it needs to consider things like the EU General Data Protection Regulation (GDPR) or the UK Data Protection Act 2018 to ensure 'consent' has been obtained. Cyber criminals simply steal email addresses and spam the entire world.

Cyber criminals aren't interested in the law (although they are interested in not getting caught!). They aren't interested in their reputation among the general public. Criminals operate with a different moral compass than the majority of society and are not fettered by the same constraints as the rest of us.

If the brain is the greatest weapon, then cyber criminals are using that against us too. They understand what drives us and use psychological tricks that leave us vulnerable and at risk of falling prey to their attacks. Cyber criminals are masters at understanding the human condition and use this knowledge against us when we are most susceptible. I often say that cyber criminals' greatest weapon is FUD: fear, uncertainty and doubt. Like hungry predators, they watch how society responds to world events and then capitalise on them. COVID-19 is a prime example of how cyber criminals adjusted their approach, launching phishing attacks, selling fake products or claiming to offer financial support during the pandemic. Knowing that the world was ablaze with FUD, they quickly 'pivoted', while the rest of society scrambled to implement contingency plans that just weren't there. As we focused on the safety of our loved ones, keeping our organisations going and holding onto our jobs, cyber criminals were sending billions of emails offering fake PPE equipment, 'mortgage holidays', tax breaks and business cash loans. All in the hope to gain access to your data.

Although criminals aren't always driven by monetary gain, it is undoubtedly a significant motivator. In legal investigations, they often say "follow the money", which is pertinent when talking about cyber crime. Hackers and other cyber criminals can earn vast amounts of money very quickly, with very little investment or effort. Because of the prevalence of data and our reliance upon it, cyber criminals know that almost every person in the world using a device is a potential 'customer', which means the cash returns are vast. It is estimated that the global financial impact of cyber crime in 2020 was in excess of $1 trillion, with some experts stating that this number is expected to rise by 15% year-on-year, costing $10.5 trillion by 2025.[7]

Cyber crime is a whole market sector and industry that we must recognise exists as a living, breathing and growing entity. It's not going away, it's evolving, and it's something we all need to recognise and understand if we are to stand any chance of not falling victim.

The threats are many, varied, and growing every day. Cyber crime has gone mainstream, and we are now faced with an

---

[7] *www.techradar.com/uk/news/cybercrime-cost-the-world-over-dollar1-trillion-in-2020*.

opponent who is highly organised and highly motivated to stay one step ahead of us and law enforcement. Cyber criminals have the advantage of not caring about health and safety or regulations and laws (except to avoid them). Without care or consideration for the end user, the sector thrives on the principle of 'develop-test-improve-repeat', at our expense. Cyber crime has reached epidemic proportions, and as we have seen, statistics of data breaches increasing exponentially with each passing year.

With the prevalence of cyber crime, you'd think that the saying "It's not a matter of IF, but WHEN" would be something we should all subscribe to. However, I think this is too negative and restrictive a viewpoint and is counterproductive; if you're guaranteed to become a victim, why bother to try to defend against it?

In truth, we should say, "It's not a matter of IF, but how prepared you are for it".

Although countless books explain how to protect our networks, systems, devices and lives, we aren't thinking deeply enough or broadly enough to be genuinely prepared for the fight ahead. We defend against unseen forces without taking the time to consider who we're fighting. We are so quick to build barriers to hide behind, but we don't know if these barriers are high, wide or deep enough to keep us protected.

We need to change the way we think about cyber security. We need to think deeper, wider and more comprehensively because cyber security isn't just about deploying the latest security tool or service. The way we are approaching modern-day cyber security is focused too heavily on technology. Although this is starting to change, there is still a compulsion to invest heavily in IT in the hope that this alone can protect us from all the problems we face. But as security technologist Bruce Schneier once stated,

"If you think technology can solve your security problems, then you don't understand the problems, and you don't understand the technology."

Cyber criminals know where our attention is, and they are masters of deception and misdirection, attacking us when we are looking the other way. They are using every trick in the book to exploit our one-dimensional thinking. The solution? We need to improve our thinking.

1: Introduction

Security and privacy in a historical context

Tracing the history of security and privacy is no easy task because, in truth, the need for both has been with us since time began. It is not hard to imagine that when the earliest cave dwellers began exploring their surroundings and found a safe watering hole, they wanted to keep that information secret from anyone else. In the age where it was the 'survival of the fittest', and knowing where the cleanest water or best food sources were was a matter of life or death, so the need for secrecy was paramount.

So the notion or idea of security and privacy have been with us since the dawn of humankind. The word 'security' comes from the Latin 'securus', meaning 'free from care'. The origin of the word 'privacy', also Latin, comes from 'privus', meaning 'single' or 'individual', with the idea that something is kept to just one individual. It's not difficult to imagine that once the earliest cave dwellers found an abundance of food, they would be 'free from care' and would want to keep this information to themselves.

Moving to more 'civilised' times, we see every major power, from the ancient Egyptians to the Romans to the Picts to the Goths, using security guards for personal protection. Over time, this extended beyond the kings and queens to wealthy people in business and families who could afford or warrant personal security, to protect what was of value.

Of course, our early history was shaped by war and conflict, and therefore the need for secrecy and privacy was of paramount importance. Ensuring your plans of attack, or how strong (or weak) your capabilities were, needed to be kept as secure as possible with the information only to be known to the very few. Various techniques were used to ensure this happened, including the use of the earliest forms of encryption. The word 'encryption' comes from the ancient Greek 'kryptos', meaning 'hidden'.

Most people have heard of the 'Caesar cipher', where words are encrypted by shifting letters in the alphabet by three characters. This substitution cipher was created by Julius Caesar in the 100 BC and used to encrypt military plans and documents. It's clear that from the earliest points of development, humankind has been keen to keep information free from prying eyes, and in many cases, this need has been a matter of life and death or national security. Lives and nations could be lost if the information fell into the wrong hands. This has held true, through every form of civilisation and era, as people continue to fight each other, and therefore the need for secrecy has never diminished. From Caesar's cipher in the 100 BC to the Enigma machine in the 20th, there has always been a need to maintain secrecy – and technological advances have helped us achieve this.

In truth, the notion of privacy and secrecy through time was of concern only for the heads of state, such as (war)lords, kings and queens, warring nations and others in positions of authority and control. The idea that the 'common man' had a right to privacy didn't arise until the 19th century when the way people lived changed due to urbanisation. Suddenly the idea that everyone had a right to privacy in their own dwelling became a genuine possibility, and the notion that a "man's home is his castle" became a very real concept.

In 1890, Warren and Brandeis published "The Right to Privacy", a law review article that made the case that every *"individual shall have full protection in person and in property"*. It is interesting to note that the article was written in response to the way the press was operating and a new technology: photography. The article states that *"It is our purpose to consider whether the existing law affords a principle which can properly be invoked to protect the privacy of the individual; and, if it does, what the nature and extent of such protection is. "*. The authors acknowledge that privacy is a fluid principle that has been reconfigured over the centuries as a result of political, social and economic change, and this is something we all should keep in mind. The concept of privacy and security is not set in stone; it is fluid and continually evolving. It must be seen through the lens of the era we are living in.

Fast forward to today. Our views on privacy and security are influenced by our environment, upbringing, belief systems and experiences. The oft-quoted "I have nothing to hide" statement is too simplistic when we consider the implications of a breach of our privacy and security. Most of us have been lucky enough to live in a society free from tyranny. We may have never been in a coercive situation or relationship. If this is true, then our views on privacy and the need for security may be relatively relaxed. However, even if this is the case, I would argue that most people have a basic grasp of privacy and appreciate its importance. Even in modern society, where people are so quick to share so much of their lives online, I would argue that there are still areas of their lives that they would rather not discuss openly. If you disagree, take a look at the following questions. Would you post the answers on your Twitter feed?

- What is your salary?
- What is your favourite sexual position?
- What is the darkest memory you have of your upbringing?
- What are your PIN code and bank details?

1: Introduction

Asking someone to share personal details about sex, money and bad memories evokes an almost visceral response. Perhaps because they are so entrenched within us, they are almost part of our DNA?

The idea that "we have nothing to hide" may be accurate, but that doesn't mean you want the world to see and know everything about you. But this is the world in which we live; a world that knows more about us than we think because our data is being used to tell a story about us. How our data will be used in the future, only time will tell.

You may have nothing to hide, and you may think that privacy is no longer the social norm (more on that later), but there is no doubt that our data is today being used in ways that previous generations could never have imagined. The question is: are we comfortable with the direction we're heading? What does it mean to society and to future civilisations? For our children? What do 'privacy' and 'security' mean in a world that is evolving at breakneck speed around us, when only a few of us are aware of the changes?

CHAPTER 2: DEFINITIONS AND CLARIFICATIONS

Those reading this book will undoubtedly be involved in cyber security and data protection, so I won't be explaining terms such as 'encryption' or 'VPN'. I have to assume a certain level of understanding, and I wouldn't want readers to think this book is for the general public – it's not. However, this said, I do believe some terms require a little exploration and explanation because they are words and phrases that are often debated, and I want to give you my take on what they mean so that we can be clear from the outset. This will help you read the rest of the book because you'll see where I stand, and then you can make a conscious decision to agree or disagree with these definitions.

Cyber

The word 'cybernetics' derived from the Greek kubernētēs, which refers to a pilot or steersman. Cybernetics rose in prominence when the American mathematician and philosopher Norbert Wiener wrote *Cybernetics: or Control and Communication in the Animal and the Machine* on control systems and communications between people and machines. He theorised that behaviour was the result of feedback mechanisms and that machines could simulate intelligent behaviour. The idea that machines could learn from constant feedback was pure science fiction in the 1940s, but we now have machine learning and AI that shows us that he was right.

While Wiener introduced the idea of 'cybernetics', fiction author William Gibson gave us 'cyberpunks', ushering in a new genre of science fiction. His book *Neuromancer*, published in 1984, introduced us to hackers and AI in a way that resonated with the public, who were fast becoming obsessed with what personal computers could do for us now and in the future.

The impact of Gibson's work cannot be overstated; everywhere you see the word 'cyber' precedes another word, it is largely down to his influence. As well as cyberpunks, we now have cybersex, cyber crime, cyberbully, cyberstalking and, of course, cyber security.

Cyber crime

Cyber crime is defined as "the use of a computer as an instrument to further illegal ends".[8] Although it's not a perfect definition, it's simple and efficient, and works relatively well, for now. In truth, cyber crime can be categorised into two distinct brackets:

1. Cyber-enabled crime
2. Cyber-dependent crime

Cyber-enabled crime describes any traditional crime that can be carried out using a digital device, thereby increasing the reach, scale and impact. Fraud, theft, provision of child sexual exploitation images, bullying, stalking, and the purchase of illegal drugs and stolen items all fall into this category.

Cyber-dependent crime is a crime that can only be carried out using a computer or other digital device. This includes the deployment of malicious software (malware) and other software (including spam) used to steal or extort money from

---

[8] *www.britannica.com/topic/cybercrime*.

individuals and organisations (ransomware). It includes carrying out distributed denial-of-service (DDoS) attacks, where 'botnets' are used to disrupt networks and bring down services.

Cyber crime has become so organised that we've seen the emergence of a new, highly organised and well-funded sector: Crime-as-a-Service (CaaS). This is where cyber criminals offer their services to others who wish to carry out a crime online.

Cyber security

In simple terms, cyber security relates to principles, practices, processes and technologies designed to protect technical networks, devices and systems from attack, damage or unauthorised access. It can and usually is a highly technical area of security, which is often left to the IT team to address. A little like the combustion engine's inner workings are left to a mechanic, users would rather not venture 'under the bonnet' as it's far too complex, and all we want is for everything to work. The idea that cyber security is a technical topic, and therefore should be left with IT is something we've lived with for more than 30 years. But this is why we're now fighting to get everyone to take the topic seriously and take personal responsibility. The idea that it's the IT department's job is still prevalent, and I've lost count of the number of times I've heard someone say, "Oh, cyber security? Yeah, that's our IT guy's job." But as technology now exists everywhere, and we're using it more and more, this is like saying it's your mechanic's job to make sure everyone drives safely!

Few people reading this would argue that cyber security isn't IT's job; we all have a responsibility to protect the data we process. Remembering that IT means information technology, perhaps we should return to a commonly used term, but one that doesn't sound quite as sexy as cyber security!

Information security

Getting back to basics is often a good thing and helps us rediscover the origins of what we do. This is one reason the origin stories of so many superhero movies are so popular; it's easy to forget where it all started. For many of us who have been involved in cyber security for some time, we will know that if we are to be truly secure, we must stop focusing and fixating on technology and look at the bigger picture: information security.

I don't know quite when it happened or how, but about ten years ago, people started talking about cyber security as if it were a new, innovative movement that everyone should be thinking about. But many of us had been thinking about the use of technology and how it relates to information security from the outset. After all, 'IT' stands for *information* technology; the means that information is controlled and processed. Technology is merely the vehicle in which information is created, moved around and shared. Information security, therefore, is the means that information is controlled and processed, irrespective of the mode of transport.

Information exists in technological form, but it also exists on paper and in people's heads. Printers and scanners are still very much in use in many offices around the world, and some industries will struggle for some time to become anything nearing a 'paperless' environment in the next 5, 10 or even 20 years. To the best of my knowledge, the legal sector and the health sector (e.g. the NHS) are still very much reliant upon physical documentation and records.

Therefore, information needs to be protected from misuse, abuse, loss or destruction in all its forms. Cyber security is a subset of information security, which can be just as complex a topic as its new, younger and sexier offspring.

Why do I refer to cyber security as being sexy? For a simple reason: I don't see many films talking about information security. The last three James Bond movies focused on cyber security and the risks posed by supervillains who could control the words vast amounts of data. Not a fan of Bond? What about the *Mission: Impossible* franchise? Still not convinced? How about *Star Wars*? If the Empire had encrypted those plans, they would never have fallen into the hands of the Rebel Alliance!

Cyber security is the new rock and roll. Often spoken about, and way cooler to discuss than information security and data protection. For many, the terms have become interchangeable. But for professionals, there are distinct differences, and each of us needs to be clear about what it is we do and how we can help people.

To put it bluntly, if you don't know the difference between information security and cyber security, you're in the wrong job.

"What I thought nursing involved when I started: Chemistry, biology, physics, pharmacology, and anatomy.

And what I now know to be the truth of nursing: philosophy, psychology, art, ethics and politics."

Christie Watson

The Language of Kindness: A Nurse's Story

CHAPTER 3: CYBER SECURITY AS AN ART FORM

When people think of cyber security, they think about networks, architecture, technology, AI and virtual reality, programming languages and protocols. But once you understand these topics, you quickly realise that cyber security and data protection are about so much more. They are about psychology, philosophy, ethics, integrity, privacy, politics and art. To put it simply, if you're devoted to the craft of cyber security and data protection, then you are an artist. Allow me to explain.

Many years ago, I was talking to a dear old friend of mine about what it was to be 'an artist'. We discussed at length how musicians, poets, writers and sculptors were artists and what set them apart from everyone else. "After all," he said, "Everyone can draw or paint, and many people can write stories or play an instrument., but few people would put themselves in the bracket of people like Picasso, Rembrandt, Da Vinci, Mozart, Beethoven, Oscar Wilde or Robert Burns." Of course, this is true, and these are not the only artists we discussed that day. We discussed Thomas Edison, Isambard Kingdom-Brunel, Alexander Bell, Elon Musk and Steve Jobs. We discussed Eric Clapton, Buddy Holly, Whitney Houston and Ray Charles. All people I would consider artists, dedicated to their craft. We also discussed what does and does not constitute art and what an artist is. The conclusion was, for me, somewhat profound and changed my views on cyber security as an art form:

"When someone works with their hands, they are a labourer. When they work with their hands and their head, they are a master. But when someone works with

> **their hands, their head and their heart, then they become an artist."**

Art isn't only about painting pictures, composing music or sculpting something. Art is any activity that you pursue creatively with the aim of producing something. I have seen security awareness programmes and compliance programmes that can only be described as artful (i.e. "full of art"). I have witnessed developers code in ways that appears to be from another dimension, with the code appearing on-screen like musical notes, and the developer's fingers dancing upon the keyboard like a concert pianist. When people ask you what you do, how do you respond? Do you say "I'm a penetration tester", "I'm a security analyst", "I'm a consultant", or something similar? Let's be clear: that is not what you do – it's your profession, but it's not what you *do*. What you do is make the world a safer place. You protect people from harm, and you take complex technical topics and help people live safer and happier lives. When people ask me what I do, I often respond along these lines, saying, "I make your life easier, so you can get on with your business while I help to protect you and all the things you love." Does that sound strange? Good. It means it's different and is likely to engage in a longer conversation about *how* I can do these things. The answer? I create art.

Artists are not just people who write poems, books and songs. Artists do not just sculpt, paint or compose music. Artists are imaginative, creative, resourceful and willing to be vulnerable or challenging. They put their hands, head and heart into what they do and put themselves on the line. Artists ask difficult questions: "Why do it that way?", "What happens if I try this?", "How can I break this?", "How can I do this differently?" Artists not only challenge themselves but also challenge us to question ourselves and our preconceived ideas. They stand up for what they believe in. They take the mundane and transform it into something new. Art is something we create when we are truly passionate about something. Artists have a vision of something they want to make, and in cyber security, that vision is often to create a safer world, for us, our families, our clients and society at large. An artist is someone who uses bravery, creativity, emotional intelligence, knowledge, insight and willingness to create something truly unique.

In his book *Excellence Now: Extreme Humanism,* Tom Peters makes a case for us all to focus on design and implores us to put design at the heart of what we do. He quotes Trappist monk Thomas Merton, who attributes the success of Shaker furniture to the creative process:

> *"The peculiar grace of a Shaker chair is due to the fact that it was made by someone capable of believing that an angel might come and to sit on it."*

How incredible is that? But why does this need only apply to carpenters? Why can't you approach the writing of a report or excel spreadsheet with an artist's mind? Why not put design and creativity into everything we do, and create something so amazing and beautiful that "an angel might" use it.

Think for a moment about the countless PowerPoint presentations you've endured. What made them painful? It was most likely how the information was relayed and how uninspiring and unimaginative they were presented. Why not create PowerPoint presentations worthy of hanging in a gallery? Of course, I'm not saying that content isn't key, because it is. But how you deliver the message is equally important.

Think of it another way: artists are storytellers. Some of the best cyber security professionals I know have a wealth of experience that they share in presentations, blogs and stories to bring this discipline to life. But other equally talented cyber security professionals I know are nowhere near as influential as those who are just better at telling stories! Storytellers share ideas and stories that inspire and educate listeners, and they tell stories that raise awareness and understanding about the need for good cyber security practices and processes.

The artist, the creator

Synonyms for an artist include:

- Creator
- Originator
- Designer
- Performer
- Producer
- Innovator
- Master

Artists push boundaries and challenge conventional thinking and the status quo. Artists are perceived as 'weird' and 'different' because they see the beauty and the detail in things that 'mere mortals' cannot see or understand. The artist is the person who stands outside, looking in through the window and imagines a different world or outcome. The artist is fearless and willing to go places or explore ideas that the everyday person can't and isn't able to.

The world needs more artists. The world needs you to be a cyber security artist.

Our world is changing. Until now, society has been built on industrial systems and processes, which we have rigorously adhered to for more generations than we care to admit. Our industrial world didn't need the kind of artists we need today, where there is no 'one solution' to a problem. There simply is no 'right answer' for every situation or issue that our current world faces. This is the paradoxical thing about cyber security: there is no such thing as 100% secure. How could there be when there are so many variables? Every person is an individual with their own drives and desires based on a unique upbringing, education and belief system. These people work in or run organisations in an array of industries and sectors, from healthcare to banking and retail to professional services. The tools and systems they use are implemented differently at every level, from country through to sector, from business to business, to person to person. But suppose we continue to take an industrial and systemised approach to cyber security. In that case, we will fail to achieve what we set out to do, which is to create something unique and highly effective for those we seek to protect.

Creating art isn't simply something we *should* be doing in cyber security; it's something we *must* do. I would suggest that once you have been in this field long enough, you will inevitably become the artist you were born to be, even if you didn't realise it.

Education kills creativity

Albert Einstein reportedly said:

> **"Imagination is more important than knowledge.**
> **For knowledge is limited to all we know and understand,**
> **while imagination embraces the entire world, and all there**
> **ever will be to know and understand."**

Teachers and lecturers will have us believe that once you have acquired knowledge and applied that knowledge, that is all that is needed to be successful. You, the cyber security professional, are artists when you see that education can only take us so far. Being creative is as important (possibly more important) than what we have learned from someone else. Cyber security professionals have learned to be adaptive and innovative, and in so doing, they are creating art daily.

Artists are leaders and 'trailblazers' who create something unique every time they engage with a piece of work or new client. This isn't to say that artists don't use techniques, tools and skills provided and developed by others – of course they do. But how they apply these tools, techniques and skills are what differentiates the artist from the masses.

Artists are creative and use that creativity to deliver something they are proud of, so they can boldly claim, "I created this!", knowing that they have produced something meaningful. The cyber security artist is the one who writes a data protection policy that fits perfectly with a young, vibrant and small company that sells cookies and cakes online. The cyber security artist is the one who helps to train 2,500 people on social engineering through interactive sessions, with stories that educate, entertain and inspire. The cyber security artist is the one who runs technical tests across the network and helps people to see the importance of secure coding practices and change control processes and procedures.

Artists take risks, are willing to make mistakes, and are happy to stand out from the crowd. Cyber security artists need to do this every day; never accepting the status quo, always ready to stand by their convictions, but without clinging to the idea that we are always right. Because often we're not. We need to embrace the fact that there is no such thing as the perfect solution, and therefore accept that we can and will make mistakes. Being 'right' or unwilling to make mistakes can be self-limiting and disastrous to us. Did Picasso stop when the time was 'right'? Or when he felt his work was done? If you're constantly worried about making a mistake, then you'll be paralysed by fear and unwilling to take action. In the words of Einstein, *"a person who never made a mistake never tried anything new."* We must be the artist who is willing to try something new.

How you see the world

How you perceive the world is how you will engage with it. I believe there is more to be gained by seeing the world through an artist's eyes rather than those of a labourer. If we feel we are part of something bigger than ourselves, then we will engage more fully in that world and enjoy the experience. There is a story that illustrates this point beautifully. It is a story told in many different ways but is a perfect example of how our perceptions colour our views.

The story of three bricklayers is a multi-faceted parable with many different variations but is rooted in an authentic story. After the great fire of 1666 that levelled London, the world's most famous architect, Christopher Wren, was commissioned to rebuild St Paul's Cathedral.

In 1671, he visited the site and observed three bricklayers building a wall. He approached the first bricklayer and asked,

"What are you doing?" The bricklayer replied gruffly, without looking up, *"I'm a bricklayer. I'm working hard laying bricks to feed my family."*

Walking on, Wren came to the second bricklayer and asked the same question. The builder responded, *"I'm a builder. I'm building a wall."* then returned to his work.

Finally, Wren came to the third bricklayer. Again he asked, *"What are you doing?"* The builder stopped what he was doing and, with an excited gleam in his eye, replied, *"I'm a cathedral builder. I'm helping Christopher Wren build a great cathedral to The Almighty."*

Another reportedly true story illustrates this point that our view of the world will determine our outlook on life. It was said that when President John F. Kennedy was visiting NASA headquarters for the first time in 1961, he came across a janitor in the hall, mopping the floor. He introduced himself to the janitor and asked him what he did at NASA. It was said that the janitor stood proudly and replied, *"I'm helping to put a man on the moon"*. Of course, this is correct, as cleanliness and hygiene in such an environment are critical to the overall mission. But it was clear that he understood how important his role was, as did the third person building the cathedral. It's just too easy for us all to forget this and forget that each of us can be an artist and remember that we can decide to see what we do as a 'job' or see it as an opportunity to create something bigger than us, something that is going to outlive us – art!

But what if what we do isn't perfect?

So what? There is no such thing as 'perfect' in the world of art, and certainly no such thing as perfect in the world of cyber security. There is no such thing as '100% secure' and no such thing as 'being compliant' either. The cyber security artist will constantly be challenged for what they do and do not do. That's why being an artist is different from being an expert – no one can argue with an expert. They are (usually) right about most things because they are basing their knowledge on facts known and understood. But as Stephen Hawking once said, *"The greatest enemy of knowledge is not ignorance; it is an illusion of knowledge."* Is knowledge enough? It can be argued that experts are not creating something that can be examined and dissected, as it is based on the pre-determined or supplied information. The work a cyber security artist undertakes will always be questioned and scrutinised and may never be fully appreciated – but that is the life of an artist. It will never be perfect, but it will be art if you deliver it with passion, drive and commitment.

> *"Correct is fine. But it is better to be interesting."*
> Seth Godin

Sadly, many people question their own abilities. Self-doubt and insecurities abound, as people tell them their work does not matter or isn't any good. In cyber security and many other professions, 'imposter syndrome' is alive and well. It's that little voice that tells you that you've got it wrong or that no one is interested in what you have to say. The voice nags at you and tells you that other people are more knowledgeable, intelligent or informed than you as you walk on stage to talk about your art. It is the voice that mocks from the sidelines of our minds, with nothing positive to say.

But remembering that nothing is perfect and that you are an artist frees you from this. It gives you the freedom to admit you do not know everything because an artist knows they do not know everything. But they do know that they can work to figure it out and create something that will work. An artist does not have to be perfect because they know there is no such thing. Being 'perfect' is a destination, but an artist is not just interested in the goal; they're interested in the journey.

In the flow

An artist will often talk about being 'in the flow', as their passion grips them, and hours melt away like seconds on the clock as they create their work. When writing this book, I recall times when I would sit down to write for 30 minutes, but that 30 minutes turned into 3 hours without me realising – I was 'in flow'. Painters, musicians and writers all talk of being in the flow and unaware of the passage of time. This may have happened to you as you wrote a blog, developed code for your business or created a policy or training programme. Your ideas may benefit one client, an entire industry or the whole world, but in the moment, that wasn't your goal or desire. Just as Beethoven or Picasso didn't sit down to create a 'masterpiece', you were lost in the work as you put your heart and soul into developing something of substance and meaning.

In his book *The Icarus Deception*, Seth Godin talks about 'kamiwaza'. This Japanese word means "god like". Kamiwaza is the destination in the pursuit of excellence, to become 'god like'. Please don't take this as believing that I or people who strive for this have some form of 'god complex'. As Godin explains, those who strive for kamiwaza ultimately reach a point of humility that they dare to *"fly close to the sun and believe they can achieve the unachievable"*. This is not arrogance. It is deceptive to believe that flying too close to the sun is the only risk; not aiming high enough can be just as dangerous! The phrase "it might not work" should be something an artist embraces because while they are right – it might not work, but on the other hand it might work, and we might create something awe-inspiring.

A core theme of Godin's book is the idea that there is humility in this level of belief and a vulnerability that we can all achieve if we strive for it. I highly recommend reading *The Icarus Deception* for further insight and inspiration on the art of cyber security.

Being willing to put your ideas and passions out there for all to see and all to critique is truly humbling and requires a great deal of bravery to be vulnerable. But remember that "beauty is in the eye of the beholder", and what you create won't be right for everyone. However, it will be right for you, or your client, or for that moment in time. The way you go about developing your security programmes or defending your systems and networks today will be different from one year ago, and it will be different next year.

To do all of this requires commitment and dedication. It requires skill, experience and a willingness to commit to your art and craft.

It's this ability to commit, to drive forward with persistence and perseverance, that separates mere mortals from those of us who are 'god like' and create art. In her book *Grit*, Angela Duckworth talks about the notion that people who have grit have developed clear goals that reflect their true desires and passions. Artists have grit because their goals are reflected in the art they create. It comes from within.

It's also worth remembering that every time you write a blog, an article, a post on social media, or a guide like this, you are creating something unique. You are creating art. Like a true artist, you are daring to be vulnerable, which is one of the bravest things a person can do.

When I work with clients, they will often ask me to help them develop policies and procedures (e.g. information security policies). Of course, I use templates, which help to ensure I'm covering all that I need. But I explain to my clients: *"What I present to you at the start is like a very fine piece of marble. It has taken years to create this marble, but my job is to sculpt it, so it becomes yours and perfectly fits your needs and vision. My skill is transforming this block of marble into something that works for you."*

You're not just an artist. You are a martial artist.

Did you know that the phrase 'kung fu' (pronounced 'gung fu') refers to any study, learning or practice requiring patience, energy and time to complete? 'Kung' can mean skilful work, hard training or endeavour, and 'fu' means time spent. Therefore, even if you've never trained in a 'traditional' martial art in your entire life, but you have dedicated your time and energy learning ANY endeavour, then you can rightly call yourself a kung fu master. Just don't go bragging in the local pub. Results may vary.

To further press the point that those of us involved in the daily battle of protecting our organisations against cyber threats and attacks, the Chinese character "mu" literally means "to stop fighting" or "to put down weapons". The word "arts" in martial arts points to skill, expression of beauty or creativity. The combination of "martial arts" could therefore be interpreted to mean ending conflict skilfully. Peace and harmony are the ultimate goals of a martial artist.

Conclusion

Anyone can get into cyber security, just like anyone can draw. But the truly great cyber security people out there are artists. They use their hands, heads and hearts to create something special.

An artist is someone who dares to destroy, rebuild and create. Doesn't that sound familiar? Doesn't it sound a lot like the hackers and cyber security exponents we come across every day? It's worth remembering that the social engineers we all fear or venerate are simply modern interpretations of the common 'con artist', the confidence trickster who uses their skills and powers of manipulation against us. Art is subjective. It is powerful and has the potential to change lives. To fully protect our world, we need to recognise the artistry in what *they do* as well as what we do.

I hope you recognise yourself in this section of the book, but don't worry if you don't. Go back and reread it again. Challenge yourself to see the bigger picture and the part you play in it. It may take imagination, but that's what's needed.

Two researchers, Zeno Franco and Phillip Zimbardo, famously coined the phrase 'heroic imagination' in 1971, stating that, the heroic imagination is *"the capacity to imagine facing physically or socially risky situations, to struggle with the hypothetical problems these situations generate, and to consider one's actions and the consequences."*[9] I believe it's our ability to see ourselves as the hero who is willing and able to take heroic action, even before action is required. Does that sound like you? I believe it does.

---

[9] *www.artofmanliness.com/character/advice/developing-the-heroic-imagination-the-5-traits-of-heroes/*.

3: Cyber security as an art form

There is an artist in each of us, and if you can't see yours right now, that's fine. They are waiting for you. If you're struggling to find them, go back through this section and take a deeper look. I promise you, they are there.

Now, let's go and explore the art of cyber security further.

Part 2: Sun Tzu's The Art of War through the lens of cyber security

CHAPTER 4: THE ART OF CYBER SECURITY

Introduction

What follows is a philosophical look at some of Sun Tzu's most famous quotes related to cyber security and data protection. Of course, philosophy can be intimidating and might be a little off-putting, but in an attempt to look at our world differently, I think turning to Sun Tzu and others will give us a new perspective on life today.

I believe there is a reason why people like Senaca, Aristotle, Socrates and Nietzsche are still so often quoted: they speak to us from across the years with words that have resonance, impact and relevance. There is wisdom in their words that we can learn from if we are willing to take the time to listen and think differently.

This section of the book focuses on Sun Tzu, who we shall meet in the following pages. His words come to us from across the centuries but are as relevant today as they were when he walked the Earth.

If you're not convinced that someone who never saw the birth of the digital age has anything to teach us, allow me to begin this section by introducing Friedrich Nietzsche (1844–1900). The German philosopher, cultural critic, writer, composer, and poet stated:

"Whoever fights monsters should see to it that in the process, he does not become a monster. For when you

gaze long enough into an abyss, the abyss will gaze back into you."[10]

There are many variations of the above, but the message is a stark warning for anyone who spends time in search of 'monsters' on the Internet, from the clearnet to the darkest regions of the darknet and the fabled 'Mariana's'.

Those who go seeking monsters be warned – for when you gaze into that dark place, that dark place will gaze back, and you may become the very monster you seek to find.

When putting together penetration testing teams and 'threat hunters', I would often have Nietzsche's words printed and placed around the office to remind everyone of the dangers of going too deep for too long. It's this kind of thinking we need to adopt. We need to learn from a variety of sources and bring their knowledge to this modern world. Remember, there is a reason they are still quoted – because they were right.

Ok. Let's meet Sun Tzu.

---

[10] Nietzsche, Friedrich, (1886). *Beyond Good and Evil: Prelude to a Philosophy of the Future.*

Who was Sun Tzu?

Sun Tzu (475–221 BC)[11] was a Chinese military general who wrote a series of letters on various topics. Arguably his most famous work is *The Art of War*. Sun Tzu lived through a period of Chinese history that was war-torn and full of political interplay, but he was a skilled strategist who helped King Ho-Lu to expand his control across China. Although we know something about his professional career, not much is known about his personal life. Some have even suggested that Sun Tzu is not just one person but several, and is more legend than an actual person. We'll leave this for others to discuss, as the focus of this guide is the idea of the 'art' of war and what it can teach us in this modern landscape. What is known is that Sun Tzu's work is more than 2,000 years old. It was (it is believed) read by Napoleon Bonaparte and other military greats and helped shape their approach to conflict and warfare. It is said that, like Sun Tzu, Napoleon understood the importance of leading people, and that people were inextricably linked to the war 'machine'. In modern warfare, many books focus on the tactics and the mechanics of warfare but pay scant regard to the humanistic side of the conflict, with both soldier and civilian considered core components of warfare.

Sun Tzu could not possibly have foreseen the dawn of electricity, let alone the rise of the IoT. But his work is as relevant today as it ever was. In fact, I would argue that it is more relevant than ever. The battlefield may have changed, but people remain the same and the need to protect our 'kingdom' is still prevalent. Our adversaries are cloaked in mystery, yet our people look to us to help them understand

---

[11] *www.britannica.com/biography/Sunzi.*

where the next attack may come from. In days gone by, villagers looked to those in command to protect the village, the castle and their valuables. An attack could come at any time, night or day, and from any direction. There were internal spies to contend with, and defences needed to be built, maintained and improved.

This speed and force of change is never-ending, nor slowing. If we build taller walls, then someone could sneak in through an unprotected gate. If we protect the gates, someone could crawl through a crack in the walls. If we build stronger defences, someone could make a horse containing a horde of highly trained soldiers to attack as we sleep. If we focus merely on the operations, we may miss the bigger picture. We need to take a more strategic approach to going to 'war', which is what Sun Tzu's work offers us.

The writer and philosopher George Santayana (1863–1952) once stated:

> **"Those who cannot remember the past are condemned to repeat it."**

So we must learn from the past for a future that is more uncertain than at any other time in human history.

Many would argue that there has been 'war' raging online since the dawn of the Internet. If we can place Sun Tzu's words into a modern context, perhaps we will find the strategies to combat unseen foes and tactics to help improve security throughout our business and personal lives.

I sincerely hope that you will get as much out of this book as I have from writing it. But please be warned: this is no 'silver bullet'. There are no guarantees in cyber security, and this book will require you to read each section, consider it carefully and apply it appropriately to your organisation or life. Simply taking the words of a 2,000-year-old military strategist and using them wholesale just doesn't work. It requires effort on your part. But I promise the effort is worth it.

Remember, you are an artist, and the art of cyber security comes with practice, contemplation and time.

This book may change your view of cyber security, your profession and your approach. I sincerely hope it does.

Translations

The most commonly used translation of Sun Tzu's work is that of Dr Lionel Giles. In 1910, Giles introduced the English-speaking world to an effective translation of *Sun Tzu Bing Fa*, literally translated as *Sun Tzu on War Methods*. Lionel Giles published his translation through Luzac and Co. in London and Shanghai under the more commercial title, *Sun Tzu on the Art of War*.

In relation to this book specifically, you'll note that Sun Tzu talks a lot about his men. Of course, in his time, the writings were aimed predominantly at men. Women were forbidden from entering the army, and any attempts to join the armed forces would be met with shame, banishment or even death. Sun Tzu's writings reflect a different time. I use his words throughout this book, but please be aware I embrace all genders and sexual orientation – to put it simply, this book relates directly to the person turning these pages.

It is also worth noting that Sun Tzu talks a lot about the 'enemy' throughout his work. During his time, the enemy was a relatively straightforward concept and identifiable entity. However, in the 21st century, the enemy isn't always so easily defined. Yes, we could say the enemy is the cyber criminal, but that is too basic and simplistic for our modern society. The enemy, therefore, comes in many forms, but in my opinion, the most dangerous enemies we must combat are complacency, ignorance and arrogance. These are as dangerous as any adversary that you'll come up against and possibly even more dangerous and frequent than any hacker or cyber criminal!

Fighting against these foes is no mean feat, but fight we must, if we are to be successful in creating a safer and more secure world to live and do business in. Seeing the enemy as the 'hacker in a hoodie' plays into the Hollywood version of what hackers are. But hackers and cyber crime are merely the symptoms of more significant problems: complacency, ignorance and arrogance. Complacent in thinking it'll never happen to you, ignorant to the actual impact a breach can have, and arrogant in thinking that you have everything covered and you're immune from attack.

There are many adversaries in cyber security, and throughout this book, I'll refer to them as the enemy (to stay true to Sun Tzu), but be under no illusion that the enemy within is just as dangerous. Keep that in mind as you turn these pages.

A new kind of warfare

In the 21st century, we are experiencing a new type of combat: cyber warfare. Organised criminals are carrying out indiscriminate attacks and focused assaults on an unsuspecting and ill-prepared world. Primarily motivated by money, they steal technology, data and information, cultivating a climate of fear, uncertainty and doubt. As we move towards a world of IoT and Industrial Internet of Things (IIoT), state-sponsored attacks on utilities and government agencies are increasingly common. The battleground is now just as likely to be virtual as it is to be physical, with software code the primary weapon of choice.

The need for cyber security is unquestionable

We are at war with an enemy that is agile and fast-moving. Of course, those at war have always embraced the latest technology to further their cause and meet specific objectives. In every war ever fought, the latest scientific advancements have been used to wage war against real or perceived enemies. From the sword to guns to aeroplanes to nuclear weapons to drones, technology is used to wage war on an increasingly remote and industrial scale. History has shown us how important technology is in warfare and it continues to be employed by governments to wage war or maintain peace. But modern warfare has moved beyond mechanical technology to computers and devices we rely upon on a day-to-day basis.

Modern warfare is not only fought in the open battlefields; it is also fought online. Our enemies know our societies are reliant upon this digital universe, and if they are able to destabilise and disrupt this universe, then they can win a major victory with the click of a button.

An example of how devastating this could be was discovered in 2010 when Iran's Natanz uranium enrichment facility was infiltrated with a computer virus (a 'worm'), which found its way onto the plant's systems via a USB stick. The virus wormed its way through networks, searching for and infecting Windows computers that ran a specific piece of software used to automate and control electro-mechanical equipment. Once it found its target, the virus recorded readings of the uranium in preparation for the next step.

The intention was to impact and degrade the quality of the uranium, so the virus began to affect the facility's centrifugal systems by fluctuating the speed at which they operated. However, before carrying out the attack, the virus recorded a 'steady state' and then went to work. Those monitoring the facility would have been shown information that the attackers wanted them to see and wouldn't suspect that anything was wrong until the equipment began to self-destruct. The uranium would be useless by that time, and the virus, Stuxnet, had done its job.

This isn't the end of Stuxnet's story. This virus is believed to have been created by the US intelligence agencies (and Israel) under the Bush administration. Stuxnet's code was released and modified to attack other infrastructure installations such as water treatment plants, gas lines, power plants and communication networks. It is thought that Stuxnet and its offspring have targeted industrial control systems around the world, infecting more than 200,000 computers and causing 1,000 machines to degrade physically.

In 2011, the report "In the Dark: Crucial Industries Confront Cyberattacks" from McAfee and the Center for Strategic and International Studies highlighted the following worrying facts:

- Extortion is the most prevalent cyber threat reported by the global energy sector.
- One in four power companies globally have been victims of extortion.
- 80% of power companies in Mexico have been victims.
- 60% of power companies in India have been victims.

- A variant of Stuxnet, "Duqu", has been reported in energy facilities in eight countries.[12]

In almost every war waged, invading armies attack water and food supplies to starve their enemies and impact the general population. In World War II, utilities and industrial cities were bombed to disrupt the war effort. In the 7th century, the Scythians employed 'scorched earth' tactics to burn crops and poison wells in the war again the Persian Achaemenid Empire. These techniques are echoed in the virtual world. Our unseen adversaries are sitting thousands of miles away, behind computer screens, carrying out attacks that can have a real-world impact on each of us.

There is a war taking place, and we have to adapt to this new battleground because each of us is a potential target. Sun Tzu's *The Art of War* is required reading for any military leader, and if we are to take the battle to the enemy, then it's essential to recognise our part in it.

Let battle commence

The Art of War has 13 chapters, each dealing with a different aspect of war. The book remains the most influential strategy text in East Asian warfare, shaping Eastern and Western military thinking, business tactics, legal strategy, lifestyles and cyber security.

The remainder of this book will focus on Sun Tzu's words that I feel are most relevant to the cyber security professional and have helped me during my career. I have interpreted his words one way, but you may find different meaning in them.

---

[12] *www.mcafee.com/blogs/enterprise/in-the-dark-crucial-industries-confront-cyberattacks/*.

If that is the case, then I have done what I set out to do: to make you think differently about our technological world and approach it with a new sense of purpose.

Enjoy the journey.

"All warfare is based on deception."

Sun Tzu

CHAPTER 5: WARFARE AND DECEPTION

This is possibly one of Sun Tzu's most famous quotes, and often quoted in relation to cyber security, and with good reason: because it is true. Remembering that their perception is their reality means you can appear stronger than your opponent, bigger and with more resources than you actually have. Thereby making it appear as if you are a more challenging target than you actually are. Likewise, those who look to cause us harm may initially be perceived as stronger and bigger than they are, or weaker to lull us into a false sense of security and complacency.

Over the years, hackers have discovered that it's easier to hack a human than a computer. After all, why spend hours breaking into a computer system, searching for a technical flaw or vulnerabilities when you can call someone and ask them for their password? Tricking users into handing over their details using a variety of techniques is the tool of choice and is played out most often through social engineering techniques such as phishing. Cyber criminals are often masters at psychological warfare and use our ignorance or complacency against us as they look to manipulate us and further their own goals. We must be on the lookout for those messages and calls that press us for information or requesting that we take action, which is often against our best interest. We need to educate our family, friends, co-workers, employees and leaders that what we see on screen isn't always true. We must be cautious when we share our data, how we share it and with whom.

Scammers and con artists have long used deception to steal from an unsuspecting public, using human nature against us.

Phishing attacks, for example, are a type of social engineering attack often used to steal user data, focusing on login credentials and banking details. They can also be used to get us to carry out instructions, such as transferring funds to a fraudulent account. The attack begins when an attacker, masquerading as a trusted entity, dupes a victim with an email, instant message, text message ('smishing') or phone call ('vishing'), convincing them to provide certain information or carry out a specific action.

Phishing attacks are on the rise; today they are the most common cause of data breaches and security incidents.[13] We therefore need to educate our friends, families and teams on the dangers of phishing. Phishing should be an integral part of any training programme, but we must include the methods cyber criminals use rather than focusing purely on the mechanisms. This means explaining how cyber criminals exploit our emotions, such as fear, love, lust, anger, greed, generosity and curiosity, to deceive us into complying with their requests. Explaining how we can be so easily manipulated and how well equipped the enemy is can reduce or remove feelings of embarrassment and shame when these people deceive us – explaining that our enemy often understands us better than we do ourselves. We must build 'human firewalls' to defend against attack, helping to protect us by protecting ourselves.

If all warfare is based on deception, in the midst of this war, we should look at how we can use deception to our advantage. Sun Tzu's advice is:

---

[13] *www.darkreading.com/edge-threat-monitor/most-common-cause-of-data-breach-in-2021-phishing-smishing-bec*.

5: Warfare and deception

> *"Hence, when able to attack, we must seem unable; when using our forces, we must seem inactive; when we are near, we must make the enemy believe we are far away; when far away, we must make him believe we are near."*

After a cyber attack or incident, there is often a desire to jump right in and fix the issue. However, this response might alert the attackers that you are on to them. It is better to tread carefully so that you have time to build an effective plan and use deception to your advantage.

> *"Hold out baits to entice the enemy. Feign disorder, and crush him."*

Using deception to your advantage could include feigning ignorance and lack of understanding of technology and creating open doors for the criminals to walk through. Many organisations create 'honey pots' to lure attackers into a trap, where they will step on a tripwire and alert you to their presence. Although this may sound like a difficult task, there are numerous tools available and straightforward techniques to help you achieve this. I have seen organisations set up drives and files that look enticing to a potential thief, such as "Payroll Data" or "Client Order Book" files. Ensuring these aren't too easy to access and implementing additional security and auditing around these areas can alert you to an intruder's presence while appearing to be in disarray.

As the saying goes, prevention is better than a cure. But if you are the victim of an attack, you can still use the art of deception to your advantage when deciding how to respond. Of course, it depends on how you became aware of the attack, but leaping immediately into action could be a mistake you live to regret. I recall being called following a breach at a company to help remediate and manage the fallout. When I took on the engagement, I discovered that the organisation had been alerted to the existence of a number of user accounts that had 'admin' privileges, but no one knew what the accounts were or who had created them. On further investigation, the organisation discovered that the accounts had been exfiltrating data for a number of weeks. The IT team promptly leapt into action and shut down the accounts. However, shortly after, the payload was activated, and data was encrypted with ransomware. This was followed by a blackmail demand sent to the CEO stating that the hackers now held all their data, and they would email the clients to inform them of the breach. They also threatened to contact the Information Commissioner's Office (ICO) to alert it of the breach. On investigation, it was clear that the hackers had been inside the systems for a considerable time. When the IT team shut down the admin accounts, it alerted the cyber criminals to the fact they had been discovered and therefore prompted them to detonate their plan.

Therefore, it is far better to consider those situations and evaluate the next step rather than immediately take action. Your actions could accelerate or exacerbate the issue, so it's essential to *respond* to an incident rather than *react* to it.

Using deception and subterfuge to lull your enemy into a false sense of security before responding will produce a more favourable outcome for you. Understanding that deception is being used as a tool against us helps us see the enemy more clearly and understand them a little better.

"If you know the enemy and know yourself,
you need not fear the result of a hundred battles."

Sun Tzu

CHAPTER 6: KNOW YOURSELF

When a good fighter steps into the ring with their opponent, they have invariably trained their bodies (and mind) as much as they possibly can. Hours of training, and eating and sleeping well, are necessary to win. But a great fighter does more than focus on themselves. A great fighter understands the importance of knowing their opponent's strengths and weaknesses so that they can exploit these when the fight begins.

This is what Sun Tzu speaks of when he suggests that it is as essential to know our enemy as much as we know ourselves.

Understanding risk

Risk management is a profession, and I have had the honour of working with, and being trained by, some incredible risk professionals. They understand the value of identifying, evaluating and managing risk. But I am often struck by the apparent lack of external risk assessment that is carried out, where the assessor will look beyond their organisation to understand what could put them at risk. For a number of reasons, identifying risks is challenging, as it takes imagination and the ability to remove (as far as possible) any preconceived ideas and biases. This is why risk management often falls short of the true intention to understand your weaknesses and strengths.

ISO 27005:2018 is part of the international information security management family of standards and is focused on information security risk management. It focuses on the asset, threat and vulnerability risk identification process, so rather than trying to understand 'risk' (which is a very ethereal concept), we must try to understand what the threat is and where we are vulnerable.

Sadly, what normally happens is senior managers are invited into a room and, without any real structure to the meeting, are asked to think of all the negative things that could happen in their departments or business. They are then asked to estimate the likelihood and then agree on the likely impact of these events. If this has been your approach thus far, just know that you are not alone, and you have most likely 'ticked a box' in a compliance checklist.

Running risk workshops is not easy and is an art form in itself. Workshops can be mundane and painful experiences, but in the hands of a true artist, they become exciting think tanks where people not only identify weaknesses but opportunities too.

This is why a risk management workshop should be facilitated by someone who understands that we're looking to identify the organisation's threats and where we are most vulnerable. The identification process should be as structured as possible. One simple approach is to focus on the following areas:

- People
- Policies
- Processes
- Physical (facilities, remote working, physical media like papers, etc.)
- PCs (systems, networks, infrastructure, etc.)
- Providers
- Parliament (local and international legislation)

As you can see, I like to start everything with the letter 'P'. Why? Because it's easy for me to remember! Feel free to substitute any of these with your own wording, but ensure you cover each asset/area in your workshop. This will enable you to quickly identify threats, which then naturally flows into the vulnerabilities, i.e. what can exploit that threat. This vulnerability is the true risk you're looking to identify.

For example:

- **People**
  - *Threat* – Competitors poaching our staff.
  - *Vulnerability* – We are not paying market rates for key staff.

- **Policies**
  - *Threat* – People breaching our policies.
  - *Vulnerability* – Our policies are too complicated and difficult to read.

- **Processes**
  - *Threat* – An accident that leads to a health and safety claim.
  - *Vulnerability* – Processes are not documented and no training is provided.

- **Physical**
  - *Threat* – Old devices are sold on eBay.

- o *Vulnerability* – No process for shredding equipment or data that is no longer required.
- **PCs**
  - o *Threat* – Cyber attack.
  - o *Vulnerability* – We do not have a patch management process in place.
  - o *Vulnerability* – No budget for new Cloud environment.
- **Providers**
  - o *Threat* – Breach of copyright or other contracts.
  - o *Vulnerability* – We do not have a list of all third parties or software systems.
- **Parliament**
  - o *Threat* – Changes in government legislation surrounding Brexit.
  - o *Vulnerability* – No contingency plans in place.

(Note that you can have more than one vulnerability for each threat identified.)

Current approaches to risk management tend to focus on the 'know thyself' part of the equation. Another simple approach to identifying vulnerabilities (i.e. risk) is to ask each senior management person what their objectives are and what will prevent them from achieving those objectives. For example:

- **Head of HR**

- o ***Objective*** – To hire the best talent and increase staff retention by 10%.

- o ***Vulnerability*** – We don't pay market rates.

- **Head of IT**

  - o ***Objective*** – To reduce outages by 20%.

  - o ***Vulnerability*** – No budget to improve technical infrastructure.

Hopefully you get the picture. This approach to identifying risks is a more subtle way to discover what people are worried about and gain buy-in. You may have read the above and wondered, *"What does hiring the best talent and increase staff retention have to do with information security?"* If you did, I respectfully suggest you're missing the point and need to broaden your perspective. In this example, hiring the wrong people could increase risks related to inadequate background checks and almost certainly will increase the amount of training you need to do – because of poor staff retention.

Remember – first, we must seek to understand, then be understood.

Under the new version of ISO 27002, a new control 'Threat Intelligence' has been introduced, which states that *"Information relating to information security threats should be collected and analysed to produce threat intelligence"*. A big part of this is the risk assessment process. Yes, there is more to gathering information on the security threats, but the risk management framework will help determine if the threat is real or not.

Where there is no structured approach to risk management, organisations will often point to technical assessments of their infrastructure. Penetration tests and vulnerability assessments are paraded as the panacea for evaluating our systems' technical vulnerabilities. Organisations might even conduct social engineering and simulated phishing attacks. Of course, all of these are great and should be employed, but they still focus on YOU and not the enemy.

Knowing your strengths and weaknesses make your organisation stronger. But considering the strengths and weaknesses of the 'enemy' is also of vital importance. Simply stating "Threat from cyber crime" or "Hackers" on your risk register is not enough.

What someone in your business needs to understand is the story behind these risks. They should be asking:

- Who are the cyber criminals/attackers?
- Why would they attack us? What is their motive?
- What information would be most valuable to them?
- What would they do with the information?
- Where would an attack come from?
- When are we most vulnerable to attack? Year end? Payday? Fridays?

That 'someone' should be you. As Sun Tzu says:

> *"If you know yourself but not the enemy, for every victory gained, you will also suffer a defeat."*

Risk management usually doesn't go into this level of detail, so you need to ask – and answer – the questions above. You can easily do this by running an exercise with your senior management team to consider these questions and then use this information to be better prepared for attack.

Finally, if you're not convinced about completing a risk assessment of your strengths and weaknesses, nor that of your enemy, consider Sun Tzu's words:

"If you know neither the enemy nor yourself, you will succumb in every battle."

So the choice is yours. To quote Sun Tzu again:

"The art of war teaches us to rely not on the likelihood of the opponent's not coming, but on our readiness to receive him; not on the chance of his not attacking, but rather on the fact that we have made our position unassailable."

"The enlightened ruler lays his plans well ahead; the good general cultivates his resources."

"If he is secure at all points, be prepared for him.
If he is in superior strength, evade him."

Sun Tzu

CHAPTER 7: PREPARATION AND EVASION

In the modern era, it is impossible to evade the enemy entirely. Automated 'bots' seek out weak and vulnerable systems/organisations and go to war on them almost without human intervention. Such is the nature of cyber warfare. Therefore, we must assume that the enemy is always willing to attack us, irrespective of who we are. If we accept this assumption and accept that they are of superior strength to us (as there is no way of knowing if they are or not), then we have no other choice than to be prepared for the battle that is sure to come.

It is not difficult to imagine that cyber criminals have read Sun Tzu, when we hear Sun Tzu state that *"rapidity is the essence of war: take advantage of the enemy's unreadiness, make your way by unexpected routes, and attack unguarded spots."* Being prepared or acknowledging that an attack is possible places us in a state of readiness that we must cultivate. However, as I have already said and firmly believe, there is no such thing as 100% secure. There are always weaknesses, unguarded areas and vulnerabilities. It is, therefore, almost impossible to be secured at all points – but this goes for the enemy too.

For example, the enemy may believe that catching them will be very difficult and bringing them to justice even harder, but it is not impossible. The international collaboration between law enforcement agencies is improving all the time. Indeed, many criminals assume they are 'secure' because of the international nature of their crime targeting one country from the perceived safety of another. Their ignorance (and arrogance?) in this area will ultimately leave them vulnerable.

However, I believe it is essential to assume that our enemy is superior in strength at an individual level. Therefore, it is better to prepare for conflict than hope we will never enter into battle. Think of it this way: if you are defending a castle, you need to have guards located at multiple points around the battlements and positioned at the gates. You'll need to ensure they are trained, well fed and motivated (or they might turn against you!). You'll need to ensure the walls and keeps are well maintained to defend against a breach in any of these places. You'll need to be constantly on the lookout and ready for attack. In 1984, UK Prime Minister Margaret Thatcher almost lost her life after the IRA blew up the hotel where she and other cabinet ministers were staying. Afterwards, a message was sent that stated: *"Today we were unlucky, but remember, we only have to be lucky once. You have to be lucky always."* These chilling words still ring true to this day in our digital lives.

There are many aspects to being prepared, and one of these is to ensure you're ready for battle, that you have accepted that the fight will take place, not that you have anticipated every move. Sun Tzu said:

"Whoever is first in the field and awaits the coming of the enemy will be fresh for the fight; whoever is second in the field and has to hasten to battle will arrive exhausted."

Being prepared means we are ready before the battle begins. In real terms, the above is good general advice. If you are going into an important meeting with the board or with a client, it is far better to arrive early so that you are fully prepared and 'fresh for the fight' rather than arrive late, exhausted and unprepared.

'Secure at all points' also means we can't simply look to the technology we use and those that support it to make us secure. We need a more rounded approach to be secure (as far as we can be) at all points. To put it simply, we need to take 'luck' out of the equation.

Information security standards can help us do this, both to be prepared for battle and to help us survive and evade permanent damage in the event of attack. Standards such as ISO 27001 and ISO 27701, the international standard for personal information management, not only look technical security but also the physical and human aspects of security. In my professional opinion, these standards are in a class of their own when helping organisations protect and prepare themselves. It doesn't matter if you are two people operating out of a rented office in Sheffield or a multinational employing thousands of staff. ISO 27001 and ISO 27701 can, if approached correctly, be applied to both ends of the scale. Both standards provide strict controls and set clear expectations across a range of areas. Under ISO 27001:2013, the controls are split across the following 14 domains:

1. Information security policies
2. Organisation of information security
3. Human resource security
4. Asset management
5. Access control
6. Cryptography
7. Physical and environmental security
8. Operations security
9. Communications security

10. System acquisition, development and maintenance
11. Supplier relationships
12. Information security incident management
13. Information security aspects of business continuity management
14. Compliance

In 2022, a new set of controls was released, which has not only restructured Annex A, but also introduced a number of new controls, which I will explore later. The new structure is based on the following four key aspects of security, rather than the 'domains' previously listed:

- Organisational controls
- People controls
- Physical controls
- Technological controls

As you can see, there is a lot more to these standards than just technology. In fact, in ISO 27001:2013 the word 'technology' appears only 11 times across 34 pages and 4,607 words. I like to think of ISO 27001 as a 'cookbook', which has a range of ingredients and recipes for you to follow (as outlined above), but YOU are the chef who must put them all together to create a masterpiece.

It's interesting that the new version of ISO 27001 adopts a model that allows more flexibility, but still demonstrates that good security is about more than just technology – it has to be organised. It needs to consider people and it needs to consider the physical environment too. If any one of these components is missing, failure is sure to follow.

There are other standards, schemes and frameworks that will help you be prepared and can even be layered on top of ISO

27001 (and ISO 27701) or used as a foundation. These include Cyber Essentials (and Cyber Essentials Plus), NIST, SANS, the Payment Card Industry Data Security Standard (PCI DSS) and SOC. Each of these merits a chapter of its own, and there is a whole body of work available to help you understand these important standards. Some might argue that ISO 27001 lacks the key controls required by these other standards, and it is too vague and open for loose interpretation. This can lead to organisations having a false sense of security about their security (!). Although I would agree to a point, I would argue that this is why you need someone who understands best-practice principles and has a pragmatic approach to implementing ISO 27001, rather than doggedly following a set of instructions.

Before we continue, I would like to state for the record that I am a big fan of following best-practice approaches to implementing standards; however, I do not think ISO 27001 *is* a best practice. For me, best practice means looking at the best way to implement something using practices that have been developed inside and outside your organisation and sector. The world-renowned speaker and author Tom Peters explains this brilliantly in his book *The Little Big Things – 163 Ways to Pursue EXCELLENCE*,[14] in which he makes the case for and against standards:

> *"I love best practices IF they are cool stuff from a dozen sources inside and outside the company and industry, available for each of us to learn from and steal from. I hate best practices when mimicry is demanded – "Do it this way, or else!" The point is this; Rigidly applied best*

---

[14] *https://tompeters.com/writing/books/little-big-things/.*

> *practice equals zero standard deviation equals regression rather than progress."*

For me, mimicry demonstrates a lack of imagination and a tick-box mentality, which we must fight against. The artist is not afraid to use their imagination and look beyond their sector and experiences to apply good security controls – aka best practice.

But I also have other concerns about some of the other standards and frameworks mentioned because they are heavily focused on technical controls. Therefore, they often neglect the importance of physical security controls, human behaviour, and data and information. Because of this, I believe that they lack the effectiveness of the ISO standards. They offer the equivalent of protecting your castle only by telling you how thick your walls need to be but have nothing to say about the guards you place at the gates.

Remember that the attacker is looking for our weak spots, and if they have studied Sun Tzu, then the following must be one of their favourite quotes:

> *"Attack him where he is unprepared, appear where you are not expected."*

While we have no way of knowing, I feel that every cyber criminal in the world must have this mantra emblazoned on their desktops.

Understanding that our attackers are looking for areas where we are unprepared and will attempt to appear in places where we least expect them reinforces the message that we must prepare for the battle ahead because a battle will come sooner or later.

Another oft-repeated phrase in the security sector is that you are only as strong as your weakest link, and in the information security profession, this accusation is usually aimed at people. I don't like this statement, but I understand what people are trying to say. People are fallible. We all make mistakes. But I firmly believe we need to consider people our greatest allies and weapons against attack. This isn't simply about training people. It's about understanding human behaviour, wants and needs, and what prevents us from being able to protect our businesses. I once worked with a company that employed more than 2,000 people, and had an 'open door' policy and operated on trust. This is a lovely idea, but based on the organisation's issues, it was clear that not every employee could be trusted. The management refused (initially) to recognise the problem and therefore were unprepared for the levels of internal fraud and issues that were unearthed when I began internal investigations and reviews.

All too often, we think of cyber security as an IT problem that requires an IT solution. This thinking is severely flawed. Consider for a moment a traditional bank robbery, where the perpetrator uses a gun to commit the crime and a car to get away. Is this now a gun problem or a car problem? Perhaps if we rid the world of guns and cars, it would end bank robbery?

Cyber criminals, of course, use computers and other devices to carry out their activities, but these are merely tools. The bank teller who has been trained on how to respond to a bank robbery is going to be a great asset, as will the shock-proof glass behind which they sit. Staff training and good strong physical security measures offer layers of protection and help you become better prepared for an attack. Cyber criminals are looking for places where you are unprepared:

people, physically, your third parties (e.g. cleaning and maintenance companies), and your processes. These are all areas that cyber criminals will consider in their preparations for an attack. Will they also use indiscriminate large-scale attacks that are less sophisticated? Yes, of course. But the successful ones will attack you where you are unprepared, and they will appear where you are not expecting them.

By employing standards to structure your defences, you create the foundation for a more successful approach to cyber security and data protection. This lack of forethought and understanding of the landscape can lead us to be complacent to the risks around us and ultimately to our downfall.

As Sun Tzu said,

"He who exercises no forethought but makes light of his opponents is sure to be captured by them."

"Just as water retains no constant shape, so in warfare, there are no constant conditions."

Sun Tzu

CHAPTER 8: WATER RETAINS NO CONSTANT SHAPE

Bruce Lee, the kung fu master and film star, is not only famous for his movies and incredible training regime, but was also a renowned philosopher who understood the importance of flexibility in both body and mind. He demonstrated this perfectly when, like Sun Tzu, he spoke of water's shape-shifting qualities:

"If you put water into a cup, it becomes the cup. You put water into a bottle, it becomes the bottle. You put water into a teapot, and it becomes the teapot. Now, water can flow, or it can crash. Be water, my friend."

Lee was stressing the importance of adapting to the environment and the conditions surrounding us. Had he been in technology, perhaps he would have been talking about our need to be 'agile' and have an agile mind, which can adapt quickly to the constantly changing environment we find ourselves in.

Sun Tzu states that:

"Water shapes its course according to the nature of the ground over which it flows; the soldier works out his victory in relation to the foe whom he is facing."

This leads us back to understanding our risks and knowing ourselves and our adversaries. As organisations become wise to what we might think of as 'traditional attack vectors' and methods, hackers will continually evolve and develop new ones to outthink us. It has become an arms race, where the enemy is constantly changing their approach based on the environment they are operating in.

An example of this is where hackers are no longer simply extorting money from companies through ransomware but also turning to blackmail, threatening to go to the company's clients to inform them that they're the victims of a cyber attack, or that they will inform the ICO of the breach.

Therefore, we must constantly evaluate the conditions around us, including the attackers' evolving techniques and our ever-changing landscape. As our businesses change and adapt to new working conditions, such as mass remote working due to the COVID-19 pandemic, we must be agile and adapt to the evolving threats, vulnerabilities and opportunities.

"Strategy without tactics is the slowest route to victory.
Tactics without strategy is the noise before defeat."

Sun Tzu

CHAPTER 9: STRATEGY AND TACTICS

Although it does not appear in *The Art of War*, this is an incredibly important quote from Sun Tzu that is worthy of deep meditation. However, I wanted to include it here because of its significance in cyber security. In truth, it should be a mantra every business owner should use.

I once met a business owner who proudly told me his business was going to be worth £5 million in the next three years, so I asked him how that was going to happen. What was his strategy? He simply repeated his statement. This is not a strategy; it's a goal. Equally worrying is the person I spoke to, who, when asked to produce their cyber security strategy, produced a statement similar to the following: *"We're going to reduce the number of incidents by 10% this year."* These are both objectives, not strategies.

To truly understand what Sun Tzu is saying, you need to understand the difference between objectives, strategies, tactics and operations. It's not just good practice, it's possibly the single most important thing you can do in cyber security and business. To explain it in simple terms, we're going to look at the analogy of becoming a martial artist.

Table 1: Strategy and Tactics

Objective	To become a black belt martial artist in under five years and be in the best shape of my life.
Strategy	Get a personal trainer and train in a martial art consistently over the next five years.

Tactics	<ul><li>Find a personal trainer.</li><li>Set annual, monthly and weekly goals.</li><li>Have a health/diet plan focused on mind, body and spirit.</li><li>Develop a series of minor milestones (to stay motivated).</li><li>Research martial arts instructors in this area.</li><li>Find a 'training buddy'.</li><li>Find an online community to share ideas and get tips.</li><li>Train on Monday, Tuesday, Thursday and Friday (2 hours per session).</li><li>Write a diet plan.</li><li>Buy training equipment for home use.</li><li>Meditate daily (10 – 30 minutes).</li><li>Develop a 'rewards' scheme for minor milestones achieved.</li></ul>

As you can see, the objective is high level but has a clear vision of the future. As you develop the ideas of *what* you want to achieve, you create the *how* and provide more details. The tactics you employ are the actual steps you'll take to achieve your overall vision.

Now let's look at what Sun Tzu is telling us, and imagine I told you I was going to do all of the following;

- Find a personal trainer.
- Set annual, monthly and weekly goals
- Have a health/diet plan focused on mind, body and spirit

- Develop a series of minor milestones (to stay motivated)
- Research martial arts instructors in this area
- Find a 'training buddy'
- Find an online community to share ideas and get tips.
- Train on Monday, Tuesday, Thursday and Friday (2 hours per session).
- Write a diet plan.
- Write a weekly training schedule.
- Buy training equipment for home use.
- Meditate daily (10 – 30 minutes).
- Develop a 'rewards' scheme for minor milestones achieved.

There is clearly a lot going on here, but is it clear what I'm looking to achieve? Would you know what success looks like? Would I know what it looks like? Is there a chance that all this 'noise' will ultimately lead to failure? Most likely. This is because I haven't set an objective and haven't set out my strategy on how to get there.

But let's look at it another way. If all I have defined is the strategy, *Get a personal trainer and train in a martial art consistently over the next five years,* but I haven't defined any tactics, then the likelihood is that I will get to where I need to be, but it will take a lot longer as I haven't defined the necessary steps to take.

Sun Tzu is telling us that if you know where you want to go but haven't planned how to get there, you will *eventually* succeed in your mission. But it will be a slow and arduous journey. Equally, if you set off on your journey with no real idea of what you're trying to achieve, then you will ultimately fail and be defeated because you won't recognise success when you get there.

I'm sure we've all seen this play out in our own lives, as people around us busy themselves with "doing stuff" and appearing very busy. Yet what they are doing doesn't move them closer to the desired goal because they haven't defined what they are trying to achieve. In cyber security, this is sometimes manifested in the spending that companies make on cyber security, as they invest in technologies and "doing stuff", which makes it appear that everything is protected. But the truth is that there is no strategy and no structure. Therefore, the programme is ultimately doomed to failure and is simply "the noise before defeat".

Developing a clear vision and a strategy is critical to effectively implementing cyber security. Before setting out on your journey, you must understand what you are trying to achieve. What are your objectives? From there, you can develop the strategies that will help you achieve these objectives, and from these strategies, you can develop the tactics (the steps) you will employ to ensure your strategies are successful.

In ISO 27001:2013, there is a specific requirement for you to identify what your objectives are. Section 6.2, *"Information Security objectives and planning to achieve them"*, states explicitly that *"The organization shall establish information security objectives at relevant functions and levels"*. It goes on to say what is expected and states that they are to be measured. This is one reason I am a firm advocate for ISO 27001 because it requires an organisation to think about what it is trying to achieve, rather than dictate a set of 'controls' that are merely the tactics used to protect your organisation.

"The art of war is of vital importance to the State.
It is a matter of life and death, a road either to safety or to ruin.
Hence it is a subject of inquiry which can on no account be neglected."

Sun Tzu

CHAPTER 10: THE VITAL IMPORTANCE OF STATE

What does 'vital' mean? It implies something that is absolutely necessary or essential to life. The word comes from Latin and means 'life-giving'.

Now you may be thinking to yourself, *"Are cyber security and data protection really a matter of 'life' (and death)?"* I genuinely believe they are. It may sound melodramatic, but the implications of poor security and lax privacy controls can be life-changing, not only on an individual level but at a societal one too. We only need to look at the Cambridge Analytica and Facebook scandal to see how data can be used against us when placed in the wrong hands.

The life and death of your business or livelihood could depend on your approach to cyber security. Those affected by cyber attack either directly or indirectly talk about losing their jobs and their businesses. They talk about the stress and anxiety caused by being hacked or having their bank accounts raided. They talk about feelings of isolation, violation and shame. Being the victim of cyber crime leaves people feeling vulnerable and risks their livelihoods, status and jobs.

In the most extreme cases, there have been instances of people taking their own lives due to a data breach. This may sound alarming, but sadly it is far more common than you'd think. Suicide is on the increase and certainly is a problem we cannot ignore in young men.[15] Place this alongside the increased use of digital devices, social media, and dating apps. It's easy to see how people can fall prey to cyber criminals and online scams that have major implications on our lives.

If there were a 'poster boy' for the far-reaching impact of cyber crime, it would be the Ashley Madison hack in 2015. There are several aspects to this story that may resonate and help illuminate our point that cyber security is too important not to take seriously.

Ashley Madison is a dating site with a difference. The site's tag line is *"Life is short. Have an affair"*. When you sign up, you provide a host of personal details about yourself, including date of birth, age, sex, sexual orientation, sexual preferences, likes, dislikes, wants and needs. On the face of it, the site exists to allow people to have casual sex and perhaps cheat on their partners. Morally you may feel this is a terrible thing, and therefore any attack on the site owners would be justified. This is something that the attackers claimed when carrying out the attack (more on that later).

However, this view may be a little too simplistic. People joining the site were not only looking to have an affair but perhaps also looking to explore an area of their lives or their sexuality that they couldn't in the 'real world'. This could be due to their religion, upbringing, career, or even the dire implications placed upon them due to their country's attitudes towards sexuality. Sadly, there are still a great number of countries where being in a same-sex relationship is illegal. For example, Section 377A is a Singaporean law

---

[15] *www.samaritans.org/about-samaritans/research-policy/suicide-facts-and-figures/latest-suicide-data/*.

that criminalises sex between consenting male adults, in public or private. The law carries with it a custodial sentence of up to two years. But Singapore is not alone in the criminalisation of same-sex relations. According to the International Lesbian, Gay, Bisexual, Trans and Intersex Association, the following number of countries have laws criminalising same-sex relations:

- Criminalisation – 2
- Up to 8 years imprisonment – 30
- 10 years to life imprisonment – 27
- Death penalty – 6 effective (5 possible)[16]

Is it any wonder then that a site that offers the opportunity to explore a side of your life that you must keep secret will attract a lot of people? Yes, affairs do happen, but the discovery of infidelity can not only lead to discrimination and personal shame. In certain circumstances it can lead to physical punishment or even loss of life. Unmarried adulterers in Saudi Arabia, for example, can be sentenced to one hundred lashes; married ones can be stoned to death.

Information on 1,200 Saudi Arabians was among the cache of stolen data from Ashley Madison.

In July 2015, the hacker group 'Team Impact' hacked into Ashley Madison's servers and stole more than 32 million members' personal details. They threatened the site owners, Avid Life Media, with the release of the information unless their demands were met. They cited moral 'outrage' that the owners had created such a site in the first place and pointed to the fact that Avid Life Media was actively selling the personal data of its members to third parties.

---

[16] *www.humandignitytrust.org/lgbt-the-law/map-of-criminalisation/*.

Depending upon your personal beliefs, you may agree or disagree with their approach and justification. That is not what is up for debate here. But the impact this had was profound in a number of ways.

First, it had minimal impact on Ashley Madison except that it brought the site's existence to the attention of millions of people who previously had never heard of it (as the saying goes, 'there is no such thing as bad publicity'). Of course, it also highlighted many other things, such as the fact that the site was not only making money from people having these extramarital affairs, but was also selling the data to third parties. These third parties could use this data to target customers with products that would be of greater appeal. It was also discovered that many of the women on the site were 'bots', and the likelihood of speaking to an actual person was relatively low. So with all of this information, you may be even more convinced that they deserved to have their site hacked and have their data stolen.

Except it wasn't *their* data. The data belonged to 32 million people who believed they were talking to other real people, with whom they could share their most profound and intimate thoughts and feelings. Almost as soon as the database was made public, account holders started receiving anonymous blackmail letters, first electronically and then physically. The letters demanded thousands of dollars to avoid having their membership made public or their infidelity exposed to their partner. Demands ranged from $2,500 to $5,000 and beyond, and made for ominous reading.

"Dear XXXXXX I am afraid this letter contains bad news. Perhaps you remember hearing in the news this past summer about a website called 'Ashley Madison' being

hacked. Ashley Madison is a website that facilitates people meeting each other that wish to commit adultery.

The hackers released the membership and billing details of all the members.

I am sorry to tell you that XXXXXX is a member of that adultery website."

The letter goes on to demand $3,500 to keep the information private, and should the letter be intercepted, there was a section addressed directly to the Ashley Madison user themselves.

One of these 32 million people was pastor and professor John Gibson. A married man with two children, Gibson committed suicide six days after the disclosure of the hack. In his suicide note, he mentioned the Ashley Madison hack and how he was "very, very sorry".

Avid Life Media stated:

"Dr. Gibson's passing is a stark, heart-wrenching reminder that the criminal hack against our company and our customers has had very real consequences for a great many innocent people."

They are not wrong. Although Gibson's suicide was the only reported case attached to the hack, it is not difficult to imagine that there were others who took the same route out of the problem.[17]

---

[17] *www.washingtonpost.com/news/acts-of-faith/wp/2015/09/09/why-the-wife-of-a-pastor-exposed-in-ashley-madison-leak-spoke-out-after-his-suicide/.*

But the Ashley Maddison hack occurred in 2015, so things must have improved now, right? Sadly not.

In 2020, news began to circulate that Finnish company Vastaamo, which provided software services to the psychotherapy industry, had been hacked. It was reported that the confidential treatment records of tens of thousands of psychotherapy patients had been stolen, with some data leaked online. In further investigation, it was discovered that the breach had occurred in 2018 – meaning the data had been at risk for two years before any action took place. In 2020, patients started to receive blackmail demands of $200 or run the risk of having their private session records revealed to the public, their employers, family and friends. It is not difficult to imagine the distress and anxiety this must have caused those patients who had entrusted their deepest, darkest and most intimate of feelings and experiences to this organisation. The head of the state digital services agency in Finland, DVV, Kimmo Rousku, said: *"The cyber-attack could have been avoided if Vastaamo had used better encryption. Management needs to wake up."*[18]

In *The Art of War*, Sun Tzu gives us this wake-up call and tells us that it is vital for the state, the governing body and those in control to be prepared (or better prepared) for what lies ahead of us. In the last 20 years of my career, cyber security professionals have been telling governing bodies, regulators, educators, business owners and business leaders

---

[18] *www.securityweek.com/private-psychotherapy-notes-leaked-major-finnish-hack.*

that cyber security and data protection are of vital importance. Only now are these bodies starting to listen.

As leaders, it is *vitally* important that we understand we have a moral duty to protect the data we are controlling and processing. Data isn't ones and zeros; it is real people with real lives. The EU GDPR has outlined the importance of completing a data protection impact assessment (DPIA). This process requires organisations to assess the use of data and evaluate the risks associated with it, paying specific attention to the impact on data subjects (i.e. people). I cannot stress strongly enough how important the DPIA is. I would encourage everyone to complete a DPIA, as it puts you in the customer's shoes and highlights your organisation's data protection responsibilities.

As leaders, we can no longer brush these topics under the carpet or devolve ourselves of this responsibility and accountability. Choosing to point at the IT, risk, compliance or legal person/department and say, *"It's THEIR responsibility to protect our data!"* is no longer acceptable (if it ever was). This is like saying to your finance team (or accountant) *"It's YOUR responsibility to save us money!"* and then spend all the company money on whatever you like! The finance team is there to advise and guide you, just as those other departments are, but they can't do this for you.

As leaders, we need to inspire others and bring them on the journey with us.

"The "Moral Law" causes the people to be in complete accord with their ruler so that they will follow him regardless of their lives, undismayed by any danger."

Sun Tzu

CHAPTER 11: THE MORAL LAW

Sun Tzu believed that the art of war was governed by five constant factors, which needed to be taken into account before going into battle. The first of these was the 'moral law'.

The moral law involves ensuring everyone involved in the battle understands why they are heading into war in the first place and the purpose behind the fight. To quote the 20th-century author G.K. Chesterton,

"The true soldier fights not because he hates what is in front of him, but because he loves what is behind him."

This resonates with what Sun Tzu said more than 2,000 years earlier, as he believed that if the people understood the morals behind the battle, they would act in 'complete accord with their ruler'.

For as long as I can recall, information security and data protection training and awareness have been seen as something to be endured; a dull, tedious experience that people dread. Like a rite of passage into the business, people sit through mind-numbing PowerPoint presentations as trainers drone on about policies and procedures. If participants are fortunate(?), they might have the head of IT or risk telling them the importance of protecting customer data. How successful has this been? Well, since we are still asking people to use 'good passwords', and we see the rate of cyber crime increase year on year, I would suggest it hasn't been very successful at all! But Sun Tzu knows why.

If we only focus on our own needs and those of the business or organisation we work in, people we hope to engage in our battle simply won't buy into the idea that cyber security is important. Organisations make great effort to explain policies and procedures that we must adhere to, yet spend little time offering context or explanation about the impact of poor cyber hygiene and data protection practices on us. And when they do focus on these things, all too often it is from the company's perspective, or worse, the impact of infringement (i.e. "it may be a disciplinary matter!").

In his book *Transformational Information Security Awareness,* Perry Carpenter discusses at length the need for greater emotional content and discourse if we are to change the *hearts* and minds of those we look to serve. He explains why so many training and awareness programmes fail, neatly summarising it into a single, simple phrase:

"*Just because I'm aware doesn't mean I care.*"

Not only is this genuinely artistic in its simplicity and approach, but it is entirely accurate. It is the piece we've been missing all along. If we explain the 'moral law' behind the fight, then we are much more likely to engage our people and garner their support for our cause. People want to do the right thing, but we have to make it easy for them and explain *why* it's the right thing to do.

How do we do this? First, let's stop 'doing' presentations 'to' people, and let's start telling stories. The world has enough facts and figures. Tell me something interesting, and I'm not talking about statistics and numbers.

How many times have we seen or presented facts that seem alarming but have little to no impact? Stating that cyber crime has increased by 650% in the past six months might be shocking – but will I join the fight to combat this rise? Doubtful. Telling someone of a data breach involving 220 million people might sound scary, but it's unlikely that we will gain the support we're looking for. It's not that people don't care – numbers overwhelm people, so statistics like '1.2 billion accounts available on the dark web' just doesn't resonate with them. The numbers are just too big to comprehend. What does 1.2 billion *look like* anyway? If people can't see themselves in these numbers, they're not likely to support your cause.

Cyber security professionals tend to rely on numbers, but I suggest that we change our approach and start thinking like an artist – let's go in the opposite direction and go small.

I'm not saying that we shouldn't use these significant statistics and numbers, because they are still relevant. But paint a picture that they can imagine and relate to. Tell them a story that makes them care about this topic. If you think this won't work, allow me to offer two options. First, you present as you always have:

"Last week, there was a breach at X, which resulted in losses of £10 billion, with a loss of 1.2 million records."

Or you could present it like this:

"Last week, there was a breach at X, which resulted in losses of £10 billion, with a loss of 1.2 million records. But the real impact was felt by customers, who were unable to access their bank accounts, people like Y, who couldn't make loan payments and couldn't buy food for her children. The real victim in this crime wasn't X; it was

people like you and me. "

Now tell me, which of these is more compelling?

Stories are far more powerful than facts. Watch any TED talk and you'll see how true this is, as we see people turn facts and figures into compelling stories, all delivered in just 18 minutes. There is also no more powerful example of taking an unpopular topic and turning it into an international movement than the 2006 film *An Inconvenient Truth* by Al Gore. It can be argued that this presentation ignited a movement for the discussion on climate change. Do you think that film would have had the same impact if Al Gore merely presented facts and figures? We cannot discuss the power of creating compelling stories that create a movement without mentioning Steve Jobs, Apple's CEO and visionary leader who dared to think differently about computing – and to get us to. Was it purely by focusing on facts and stats? The dimensions of the iPod and the amount of storage? No. He created a vision we could buy into. He was a master storyteller, and his talks started a 'movement', and supporters of Apple products are almost evangelical about them. That couldn't happen with facts and figures alone.

It's worth remembering that we have been told stories from the youngest age to emphasise a moral imperative. For example:

- **The Boy Who Cried Wolf** – liars will not be rewarded.
- **Chicken Little** – believe in yourself, even if you feel the sky is falling in.
- **The Emperor's New Clothes** – don't let pride keep us from speaking up when we know the truth.

If I was to ask you to watch a presentation about a data breach that could cause the loss of an entire operation, you might be vaguely interested. But what if I told you it was about a young princess who was part of a rebel alliance who had managed to steal the plans to a destructive weapon? Which do you think would be more compelling? The moral of the story behind *Star Wars: A New Hope*, is that people working together, with faith and self-belief, can overcome a technologically advanced enemy (that sounds familiar, doesn't it?).

Consider for a moment that behind every great story is a moral dilemma. The love story where the protagonist is tempted to cheat on a loved one but didn't. The hero who is tempted by 'the dark side' but ultimately decides on a different path. The authors of these tales take us on the "hero's journey", and there is a moral to the story that speaks to us personally, and we 'feel' the pain of the hero, and we are 'on their side'.

Sun Tzu tells us that we must ensure we articulate the moral law so that people understand and resonate with them. We need to contextualise and reframe cyber security and data protection so that people understand what it means to them personally. Only then can we begin to explain the wider implications and expect them to participate and engage in our organisation's protection. I believe the moral law, and therefore the hero's journey, is as follows:

1. Cyber security in a personal, individual context.
2. Cyber security in a family context.
3. Cyber security in a business context.
4. Cyber security in a societal context.

As previously stated, most organisations only focus on cyber security in a business context (the third level). If this is your approach to cyber security training, it's likely you'll never get the support you need. However, by using all four of the above steps, people will begin to understand the real-world implications of their actions. From this point on, I urge you to give up on the notion that you are giving a presentation on cyber security, in favour of telling stories. Presentations tend to be devoid of emotion and only focus on facts and figures. Cyber security is full of stories, which only a very few people use in their training sessions. Even when they do, they focus on stories from a company perspective. For example, we talk about the breaches of TalkTalk, BT, London borough councils, British Airways, the NHS, Facebook, etc. But where is humanity in this? What about the couple who lost their life savings because their law firm was hacked? Or the businessperson who lost their company due to ransomware? Yes, we should back up what we're saying with facts, and we can explain things that make logical sense, but if you want your message to stick, if you want people to follow you, you need to appeal to the emotional side of their brains first.

Start thinking of yourself as a storyteller, not a presenter. People are far more likely to support your cause if they understand where they fit into the story and see themselves as part of it. By reframing this as a hero's journey where they have a chance to impact society at large, you're more likely to gain their support.

Sun Tzu felt it was important that people understood the moral law, even though he was talking about troops, who could quite literally 'face the chop'! You'd think that fear alone would ensure compliance (which is what a lot of cyber security practitioners believe, too!). But he knew that he needed every person to fight to the bitter end in a war, and he knew that desertion was a genuine threat too. Far better than compliance is to gain support by explaining the bigger picture and the cause you fight for. People are far more likely to follow you when the cause is bigger than themselves. This is extrinsic motivation (external) rather than intrinsic (internal). We see this many times in life, where people who would never run a mile will run a marathon for a charity they support. They are no longer running a marathon; they are running to help a cause. If they simply decided to run a marathon, with only the desire to be healthy (internal motivation), they are likely to give up the race. But because they understand the 'moral law', they are likely to stay motivated.

Start with why

There is a fantastic business book written by Simon Sinek called *Start with Why*. Sinek asks why some people and organisations are more inventive, pioneering and successful than others. And why are they able to repeat their success again and again? He answers this question in a variety of ways but ultimately concludes that it's because, in business, it doesn't matter what you do; it matters why you do it (there is more to the book than this, so please read it).

Think back to when you were young and your parents would ask you to do something. If you were feeling brave, your response might have been, "Why?". Perhaps the reply came back "Because!". Anyone with children will tell you that kids want to understand why things are the way they are. They want to know why the sky is blue, what clouds are made from, why you don't fall off the planet... the plethora of questions can feel infuriating! There is even a Japanese business principle based on the '5 whys', which originates from the way children ask so many questions. The basic premise is that if you ask 'why' five times, the likelihood is you'll come up with the truth or the core of an issue. It's a business principle worth thinking about because it can effectively get to the heart of a problem very quickly. But for now, let's simply stick with the notion that without understanding why something must be done, the likelihood is that people won't do what you're asking. This is the same in cyber security and data protection as any other walk of life; if people don't know why cyber security is important, they'll likely pay little more than lip service.

By helping people understand why cyber security and data protection are important (the moral law), you are more likely to garner their support. They will follow you (and your instructions) regardless of their personal wants and needs. If you do it well enough, perhaps they'll follow you regardless of the dangers they face themselves.

"Now the general who wins a battle makes many calculations in his temple ere the battle is fought.

The general who loses a battle makes but few calculations beforehand.

Thus, do many calculations lead to victory, and few calculations to defeat: how much more no calculation at all!

It is by attention to this point that I can foresee who is likely to win or lose."

Sun Tzu

CHAPTER 12: CALCULATIONS IN BATTLE

When it comes to waging battle, it is vital to calculate many things before entering the fray. Everything from the cost of food (for the troops) to munitions and soldiers' costs must be considered. In centuries gone by, if the battle was overseas, estimating how many soldiers could be lost on the journey was a key consideration, or the battle could be lost before a single shot was taken.

In modern times, and in business in particular, we know the benefits of planning. We might spend time with business coaches who impress upon us the importance of developing clear goals and strategies. Calculating the cost of business can play an instrumental role in our success.

But while we are calculating the cost of business, these preparations often don't include any formal approach to risk management. This is in spite of the fact we hear how people have taken 'calculated risks' when launching a business or a new product or service. When someone says this to me, I wonder what their reply would be if I asked them to show me their calculations. I doubt many could produce anything of meaning. This is because invariably, people haven't made any. They may have some vague notion of an idea and then immediately swing into action in the hope that everything will work out just fine. Of course, the more established the business, the less likely this is to be the case. But certainly, when working with entrepreneurs, start-ups and small businesses, the truth is that many simply haven't done the calculations that are required to ensure success.

We are talking about the kind of calculations that directly impact cyber security and data protection; this is the calculation of risk. Often referred to as risk management, it's important to consider (i.e. calculate) what risks are present by setting out on a specific course of action. Remembering that 'risk' can be both positive and negative, it is crucial that we see risks as a fundamental part of success or attaining 'victory'.

In the ISO 27001 standard, understanding risks and having a defined risk management methodology is a mandatory control and is often seen as a fundamental basis for the whole management system. 'Thus, do many calculations lead to victory' when implementing the Standard.

For those new to the idea of making such calculations, it is crucial to calculate the likelihood of an event occurring and its impact. This sounds easier than it is, and once you try doing it, you'll quickly see why so many people ignore this critical task. The perception of risk is difficult to nail down because it is a 'perception'. It is ethereal and often complex to clearly articulate, let alone calculate. When it comes to calculating risks, it is usually based on estimates and 'gut feelings' unless there have been incidents that have already had very real-world impacts. But even then, our perception of risks is skewed. For example, if I were to ask you the likelihood of another pandemic occurring, you might say the risk is high. This is because we have all just experienced a second, third and fourth wave. However, if I was to ask what the likelihood was of suffering a cyber attack, you might say it was low – but only if you haven't already experienced one. It's worth remembering that calculating risks is complex because risk perception is highly personalised. It is generally based on our experience, training, knowledge and even belief systems, which gives each of us our 'risk personality'; to put it simply, some of us are risk averse while others are risk-takers.

12: Calculations in battle

The key point to note is that it is vitally important to calculate the risks associated with cyber security and data protection. This isn't only looking at the risk of cyber attacks but includes calculating risks related to projects and business changes. Calculating risks will help you prepare for what might occur, reduce the likelihood of adverse effects or reduce the impact should they occur.

As Sun Tzu said, where few calculations have been made, we can usually see why the battle was lost. If no calculations are made, then the loss is all but guaranteed.

"Now in order to kill the enemy, our men must be roused to anger; that there may be advantage from defeating the enemy, they must have their rewards."

Sun Tzu

CHAPTER 13: REWARDS OF WAR

Let's be honest, those of us whose job is cyber security and data protection often feel it is a thankless task. So imagine what those outside our profession feel when faced with the task of implementing these disciplines into their organisations. If your business is never hit by a cyber attack or suffers a data breach, then people wonder what the fuss was all about. We are accused of scaremongering, catastrophising – at the very least, you are seen as someone who is a little 'paranoid'. But if nothing ever happens, the board will wonder why they're investing money in this area and may even think about making cutbacks in the budget. To put it simply, if nothing happens, no one knows you exist, and if you predict future events, there is a strong chance you'll be accused of suffering from the 'Cassandra effect'. This relates to a person whose valid warnings or concerns are disbelieved by others. The term originates from Greek mythology, where the King of Troy's daughter, Cassandra, was given the gift of prophecy by the god Apollo. But when Cassandra rebuffed Apollo's advances, he placed a curse on her so that no one would believe her even though she was able to foresee the future.

However, the minute something happens, such as a breach or cyber attack, you are in the spotlight, and people want to know why you didn't do more to prevent it. Why did you allow this to happen, and why didn't you warn people about it? (Even though you probably did!)

Sun Tzu states that people must be 'roused to anger' to kill the enemy, but this wouldn't do you much good in the board room or general business discourse. But being 'roused' can also be seen to mean 'excited'. If we can get people excited about cyber security and data protection, then the chance of support for these topics is significantly increased. We'll return to this shortly, but let's stay with Sun Tzu for a moment and the idea that people must have their rewards.

The blame game

All too often, when there is a breach, the natural inclination seems to jump straight to who is to blame. While this is part of the initial response (to some extent), it is not helpful. The question should be "What has happened?", quickly followed by "What must we do now to address the issue?". Knowing how it happened is an essential step in the incident management process, but focusing on blame will only do one thing; drive people underground. This is one of the reasons that in most cases, a 'chief of...' cannot be a data protection officer; There is a conflict of interest following a data incident, as there is a chance the 'chief' would not disclose the issue, should one arise.

Of course, there must be repercussions for a clear breach of data security practices and dereliction of duty. One can only imagine the forms of punishment meted out in Sun Tzu's day, but in the main, it is not helpful to vilify or play the 'blame game'. In recent years, the term 'victim blaming' has become a generally accepted phrase to describe the act of blaming (and sometimes shaming) people who have become the victim of crime. Blaming the victim is nothing new; criminals have long used excuses such as *"They shouldn't have made it so easy for me to steal it."* But it seems this practice has seeped into the office space, and when people click links in phishing emails, we see them punished for not being aware or vigilant.

If we are going to change the story, we need to begin to replace the stick with the carrot. We need to think about the rewards for helping to repel the enemy, and these rewards should be included at different levels throughout the organisation. From the boardroom to the cleaning staff, everyone should receive reward and recognition for playing their part in protecting the organisation. What form this takes depends on your organisation, but typically I have implemented reward schemes for the following:

- The best idea to improve cyber security and data protection.
- Examples of cyber security risk management in a project.
- Most improved functions (e.g. reduction in data use/retention).
- Reduction in cyber security incidents.
- Most questions asked during training sessions.
- The best cyber security and data protection project.
- The best idea to raise awareness of cyber security and data protection.
- The most significant contribution to cyber security and data protection.

I also feel that following a significant incident or event, those directly involved in cyber security and data protection must receive some form of reward or recognition for their efforts. During the 'root cause' process, I look to identify the 'heroes of the day' and ensure they receive the recognition they deserve. This can be as simple as a 'Thank you' from the CEO, which is publicly shared, all the way through to time off, to a monetary reward. The point is that there is some form of recognition (or reward), and others see it as a positive endorsement, which will rouse them to action.

Rousing the C-suite to action

Anyone involved in cyber security and data protection for any length of time will tell you that prior to an incident occurring, gaining any time with the board or increasing the budget is almost impossible. But following the incident, there is a focus and attention like never before. This is because they have (finally) been 'roused to action'. They must now attempt to fight the enemy that is upon them. So, in order to 'kill' the enemy, people must be roused to action before the attack takes place. For this to happen, they need to see the advantages of defeating the enemy and the rewards from their efforts. Looking at the board, we need to consider what motivates each person sitting around that table; what advantages are there personally in defeating the enemy? We need to be clear about the rewards they will receive for being 'roused to action'.

For example:

CEO – Chief Executive Officer

1. Increased profitability
2. Reduced costs and overheads
3. Brand and share value protection

CTO – Chief Technology Officer

1. A reduction in incidents reported through to IT
2. A clear understanding of what systems are critical
3. Increased productivity and uptime of critical systems

COO – Chief Operating Officer

1. Increased productivity
2. Reduction in employee turnover
3. Reduced costs

CFO – Chief Finance Officer

1. Reduction in costs
2. Increase in revenue
3. Share value protection

CSO – Chief Sales Officer

1. Business differentiation
2. Increased sales
3. Reduction in sales cycle

CHRO – Chief HR Officer

1. Increased staff retention and engagement
2. Reduction in staff absenteeism
3. Increased productivity

Thinking about the rest of the organisation, the following shows that there are rewards for everyone, which should rouse them to action.

All staff

1. Increased productivity
2. Protection of employment
3. Career advancement

You may disagree with some of these 'rewards', so feel free to decide your own. You may also note that I have neglected to include the CISO, or anyone from legal, risk or compliance. The simple reason for this is that the rewards for these people are typically well understood, and indeed YOU may be the CISO and therefore have no need for rewards to act. The key point is that you identify the rewards that will benefit people going into battle with you, and you identify the rewards that mean the most to them. Gone are the days where we dictate a policy and hope for blind obedience and compliance. Even during a time of great compliance and obedience, Sun Tzu knew the benefit of rewarding his men so that they would be roused to anger/action:

> *"When he utilizes combined energy, his fighting men become as it were like unto rolling logs or stones. For it is the nature of a log or stone to remain motionless on level ground and to move when on a slope; if four-cornered, to come to a standstill, but if round-shaped, to go rolling down. Thus the energy developed by good fighting men is as the momentum of a round stone rolled down a mountain thousands of feet in height."*

"Thus, the good fighter is able to secure himself against defeat but cannot make certain of defeating the enemy."

Sun Tzu

CHAPTER 14: GOOD FIGHTERS

Despite everything that Sun Tzu wrote about securing victory in battle, he recognised that there are no certainties in war, even for a 'good fighter'. Similarly, we need to remember that there are no guarantees with cyber security and data protection. There is no such thing as '100% secure', and anyone who tells you differently is lying. This is something I tell my clients all the time.

No amount of policies, firewalls, malware protection, Intrusion Detection Systems (IDS), Intrusion Prevention Systems (IPS), and training and awareness will give you 100% security; it simply doesn't exist. There are simply too many variables. This doesn't mean that we shouldn't do all we can to protect ourselves because, of course, we should. It's correct that we invest time and resources in developing our defences, including writing policies, installing firewalls and malware protection and training our teams to be on the lookout for scams. If we don't do this, then the likelihood of becoming a victim of cyber crime is significantly increased.

Although there is a touch of inevitability in this thinking, I am not, as I mentioned earlier, a prescriber to the thinking that, in relation to cyber crime, it's a matter of when not if. I do believe some of us will go through life without becoming the victim of cyber crime, but let us be honest for a moment – the odds are stacked against us. Cyber crime is on the increase. Our reliance on technology is on the rise. Our creation of data is on the increase.

Go online and search for the following questions:

- How many devices are there in the world?

How big is Cyber crime in [name of country]?

• How much data is there in the world?

Also consider for a moment the number of online accounts you have. Write down all the devices you use in your personal and professional lives that can collect information (this includes all those devices classified as 'smart tech'). Everything from TVs, game consoles and cars, to the heating and security cameras in your office collect data about you and those around you. Now do the same for all the services and systems that you access via login page. This includes shopping, banking, gaming, dating, utilities, education and social media sites. Now think about how many variations you have, i.e. if you have more than one bank account or credit card or have changed banks recently, then these need to be factored in. It's not unusual to quickly get to 30 or 40 different online accounts, yet we're still downplaying the risk of a cyber attack or data breach. Like it or not, our digital footprint is there, and it's there for anyone to use if they can gain access to it.

Even those who believe they have removed their online presence as far as possible still have a digital footprint. It's simply unavoidable. Remember, even if you never use social media, those around you probably do, and if you've ever been 'snapped' in a group selfie, then you do exist on social media. Your data sits on an electoral register somewhere, and as the banking moves inextricably towards 'open banking,' it will only increase our footprint. Even our children have a digital footprint even before they touch a digital device; from the NHS and healthcare they receive through to the schools they attend, someone, somewhere has a digital profile of your child.

The above information may not be news to you, If that is the case, I would ask you to use this information in your training and awareness programmes or as an exercise in class to illustrate just how big the problem is. To put it simply, if our online lives were a castle, the castle has grown 400 times bigger than it was five years ago, and we haven't increased the number of security guards helping to protect us.

I could go on, but I think the point is made. Like it or not, we have a digital identity that needs to be protected. Although I don't prescribe to the notion that an attack is inevitable, I don't blindly ignore the risk either. In the same way that I don't leave my house without closing the windows and locking the door, I make sure that I've stacked the odds in my favour to repel any online thief too.

Defeating the enemy cannot be guaranteed, but this doesn't mean we concede defeat and accept that if an attack happens, we'll lose. We should do all we can to secure ourselves against an attack and have good plans in place should it happen. That's the sign of a good fighter – recognising that there are no guarantees of winning, but doing all they can to secure victory. As Sun Tzu puts it:

"What the ancients called a clever fighter is one who not only wins but excels in winning with ease. Hence the skilful fighter puts himself into a position which makes defeat impossible and does not miss the moment for defeating the enemy."

"Fighting with a large army under your command is nowise different from fighting with a small one: it is merely a question of instituting signs and signals."

Sun Tzu

CHAPTER 15: SIGNS AND SIGNALS

Over the years, I have successfully implemented cyber security and data protection compliance programmes in organisations that employ thousands of people, with offices and services that stretch across the globe. I have also worked with small start-ups made up of just two or three people. Irrespective of the client's size and complexity, my energy, enthusiasm and excitement do not differ, but my approach does.

I often hear cyber security practitioners complain that implementing compliance programmes within larger organisations is more difficult, but as Sun Tzu observes, success is merely a question of instituting signs and signals. I'm sure we've all come across the organisation that is simply 'ticking a box' or paying 'lip service' when it comes to cyber security and data protection. Suppose this is the organisation that you're working for. In that case, it will become increasingly difficult to implement a robust compliance programme because the signs and signals coming from the head of the organisation are that this is a topic that isn't important. We need visible support from those who lead our organisations and a clear demonstration that cyber security and data protection are of critical importance.

When I say 'visible demonstration', I'm not simply saying that the head of the organisation sends out a firm email of support or stands up in a presentation and talks about the importance of these topics. Although this is helpful and should be conducted, I believe more subtle signs and signals are required yet often ignored. For example, if your policy is not to allow BYOD (bring your own device), yet the CEO and head of HR bring their own laptops, then you are sending a clear signal to the business that it's one rule for them, and another for everyone else. Suppose your security programme states that training and awareness are mandatory for all staff members, with the caveat that the senior leadership can 'skip' the training. What message is that sending to your teams?

You're saying that policies aren't important and can be broken. You're implying that there is a difference between the 'rank and file' and those in command. These are dangerous messages to be sending out, irrespective of your organisation's size and complexity. It's crucial to ensure that everyone (in managerial positions) supports the security programme. Although it may take longer for the message to filter down in larger organisations, it must still be seen as a priority for everyone. Although some will argue that the larger the organisation, the more difficult this becomes, I disagree. It becomes more critical the larger the organisation, and the only difference is the time it takes to implement the programme. It takes longer for the signs and signals to be seen and understood, so you need to break up the problem into smaller sections. As the saying goes, "How do you eat an elephant? One bite at a time". Sun Tzu puts it better:

"The control of a large force is the same principle as the control of a few men: it is merely a question of dividing up their numbers."

When looking at the organisation, you should study the organisational structure to understand how to divide its numbers. If the organisation is relatively large and spread geographically across many regions, what does each region look like? Is there a 'head of' for that region? Is there an office manager for each location? If there is, then that's the person you must engage with and convince to support what you're trying to do. This is vitally important if you are to be successful because it is likely that they will have their own way of doing things. It's important to remember that every region is different, and this point is especially critical when the organisation is spread internationally. Attitudes, experiences and beliefs change from location to location, and if you're going to be successful, you need to appreciate this and respond appropriately.

I was once asked to implement a business continuity management (BCM) programme across a number of European countries and was given a relatively short time frame in which to do it. I had the necessary BCM knowledge, but how to would I deliver this across 15 countries? The first step was to understand organisational structure at each location: who were the 'heads of', and what functions operated in these regions? I then examined how these regions had been operating; Were they successful? What issues were they having? Once I had a handle on this, I arranged one-to-one meetings with regional leaders (via video/phone) to understand them and their attitudes towards this discipline. I wanted to know what had gone on before and why they felt the BCM programme had failed. I asked them what they would *not* like to see from me and how I could ensure success in their region. The answers differed greatly from region to region and enabled me to adapt my approach according to the information I had obtained. Furthermore, it meant that the head of the operation understood what I was trying to achieve on behalf of the organisation and was far more supportive than they would have been previously. They were visibly supportive in the programme, signalling to their teams that this topic was important and needed their attention. As always, there were 'bumps' on the road, but the programme was a success across all regions.

Even when the organisation is small, you need to think about the 'heads of' for each function and get them onside so that they signal to their teams that you are worth listening to and following. This approach is far more successful than simply asking the CEO/business owner to email everyone to tell them that cyber security and data protection are important (yes, this is a great idea, but the bigger the organisation, the less effective this approach is).

There is a subtlety to this. Putting in place cyber security and data protection processes takes planning, persistence, imagination, tenacity, emotional intelligence, and a whole heap of energy. These qualities are separate from the technical knowledge and skill that a good practitioner will embody, which is why finding someone skilled in this area is difficult. I've met and worked with people who are skilled technically at cyber security but have no emotional intelligence, and therefore lack the social skills to empathise with those they seek to protect. Furthermore, they lack the energy required to engage with more extensive programmes and clients. They are happy in their sphere of influence (aka 'bubble') but lack the capability to see beyond the narrow confines of their comfort zone. They often grow frustrated by the lack of understanding of the end user, and the end user becomes frustrated with the lack of engagement and progress.

To be truly successful in implementing cyber security and data protection practices, those who lead must signal its importance to their teams. These leaders must be converted into advocates and supporters of what you do, and the way you do this is with emotional intelligence, paying attention to both logic and emotions.

"In war, the general receives his commands from the sovereign."

Sun Tzu

CHAPTER 16: THE GENERAL AND THE SOVEREIGN

In the day-to-day operation of an organisation, information is cascaded and escalated daily, usually without much thought. Commands come down from the head of the organisation, and we follow them to mutual satisfaction. However, during times of war or crisis, these chains of command can sometimes become fragmented, as well-meaning individuals try to help. Sun Tzu implores us to remember that we need to listen to the head of the organisation and receive commands from them.

One of the key aspects of incident management and business continuity that is often forgotten is identifying an 'Emergency Management Team' (EMT) and having clearly defined roles and responsibilities for them. You can also call the EMT the crisis management team or incident management team – that decision is yours to make – but all team members must know what role they are likely to play if there is a crisis.

The team provides advice and guidance based on their knowledge and area of expertise. They will be responsible for assisting in the recovery of the organisation using these skills, which is vital if there is to be a fully rounded emergency management team. Team members typically include:

- EMT leader
- HR
- IT
- Operations

- Compliance/risk/legal
- Facilities
- Finance
- Marketing/communications

Other than the leader, there is no one person more important than the next, but each area must be represented on the EMT. Based on the specific nature of the crisis, the team may be fully formed or a subset of the whole.

If yours is a small organisation, then you may argue that the above roles do not exist, but I would counter by saying that in a crisis situation, the above responsibilities need to be addressed by someone. Therefore, even where a company may not have a 'head of HR', someone needs to be responsible for considering the 'people issues'. Suppose you are in rented offices, and therefore don't have a 'head of facilities'. Someone will still need to consider the facilities you might need in a crisis. This could include identifying new premises, redirecting the post, increasing security (at the recovery site or affected site), and cancelling the milkman!

The EMT's purpose is to ensure the head of the organisation has all the facts, figures, and information they need to make an informed choice and then issue commands based on this information. This is an essential point to consider. The most successful sovereigns throughout the ages have recognised the importance of having advisors around them who could give them reliable information upon which to make their decisions. This hasn't changed. Leaders need people who can advise them and provide accurate information on the unfolding situation.

I once worked with an organisation that experienced a severe outage at its primary data centre. The outage took out all services for more than 72 hours, leaving the organisation's customers quite literally in the dark. As the organisation's contingency plans kicked in, I noted the EMT was missing one vital element: human resources. I requested that we appoint an HR representative to the team to advise on people issues and provide oversight on the recovery. To bring services and systems back online took several days, and during that time, the most significant challenges we faced were focused on ensuring people welfare and communication. The HR representative highlighted the need to ensure people took regular breaks, that we weren't over-reliant on one person working extended hours, and that teams were regularly briefed to reduce anxieties when dealing with angry customers. Had this incident been dealt with as a purely IT issue, the recovery could have looked very different. At one point, the IT leader proudly stated that one of his team had "worked through the night", but the HR lead asked that this person be relieved of their duty, as there was a risk they could make an error due to fatigue. Additionally, the HR lead was the one who explained to the EMT leader the importance of keeping all team members updated (on an hourly basis) on the recovery effort so that they had the latest information to relay to customers.

The outcome of the crisis was that employees felt involved and informed throughout, which made their jobs easier. Customers were not given some vague apologies and excuses but kept fully aware of the situation. Social media was used to provide general updates and updates on the recovery effort, and although (predictably) there were some negative comments, the overwhelming response was one of support.

Did this happen because the EMT leader did it all? No, but they made important decisions based on a fully rounded team. To put it simply, the leader does not know everything. A good leader makes *decisions* based on the EMT's information, and a good EMT will follow those instructions for the benefit of all.

"A soldier's spirit is keenest in the morning; by noonday, it has begun to flag, and in the evening, his mind is bent only on returning to camp.

A clever general, therefore, avoids an army when its spirit is keen but attacks it when it is sluggish and inclined to return. This is the art of studying moods."

Sun Tzu

CHAPTER 17: THE CLEVER GENERAL

It is difficult sometimes to engage organisations in discussions around cyber security and data protection. How can we make this easier for ourselves? One method is to take extra care in selecting the time of our engagements with individuals and teams.

This might lead to greater success in garnering support for what we do. Sun Tzu said that the spirit is keenest in the morning, so perhaps that's the best time to run your next cyber security training programme. I have always found running sessions in the morning to be far more successful than later in the day. Avoiding Mondays and Fridays is also a good idea. On Monday, people are readjusting after the weekend and return to an inbox that requires their immediate attention. On Friday, people feel jaded, tired or distracted by the upcoming weekend. In both situations, the likelihood is that their attention will flag when you need it to be at its highest. In my experience, holding training sessions or meetings on Tuesday or Wednesday morning seems to work best.

But it's not just training sessions that you should time carefully. If you're presenting to the board and need a decision from them, your pitch's timing could be fundamentally important to achieving your desired outcome.

Decision fatigue

Believe it or not, we all make thousands of choices each day. Some may not register as a choice, but still, choices they are. From the mundane, what to have for breakfast and what shirt to wear, to the more important decisions of which email to answer first, and what project requires our focus. All these decisions can ultimately lead to something called decision fatigue. This term was coined by social psychologist Roy F. Baumeister, who first recognised the emotional and mental strain resulting from a burden of choices. If you're wondering if this is a real phenomenon, then let me ask you this question: have you ever stared at the TV screen, scrolling through the hundreds of TV channels thinking, "There's nothing to watch!"? If you have, then you have just experienced decision fatigue. There are hundreds of shows to watch, but you can't decide which because there are just too many options. In another example, restaurants have long recognised the problems caused by decision fatigue, which is why 'posh' restaurants will only have a small number of choices. It's not just about quality is better than quantity; they understand that people become overwhelmed when faced with a wide variety of choices.

What does this have to do with cyber security and data protection? Simple: do your best to get in front of decision-makers before they become fatigued. If you're presenting to the board about a new initiative or technology you want their endorsement on, don't simply ask to be put on the agenda. Find out when the meeting will take place (preferably in the morning) and get yourself as high on the agenda as possible, and present only one or two key ideas and initiatives you need a decision on. If you are the 20th topic in a meeting that has been running for three hours, and you have five or six options for them, the likelihood is that the board members are going to be tired and suffering from decision fatigue. Take into account their mood and decision-making capabilities because irrespective of how mature and experienced they are, we are all human and suffer from the human condition. What you are learning here is a very subtle form of human hacking, something social engineers have been good at for a long time. Let's explore this a little further.

The human condition

The fundamental basis for most cyber attacks is the exploitation of the human condition. For a long time, we thought that all we needed to do was improve our technical security measures, and we would be protected from all attacks. But this was never the case, and cyber criminals have known this from the outset. Thieves, con artists and scammers have been with us since the dawn of time. Although their mode of operation (MO) may differ depending upon the time we're living through, these conmen have always looked to exploit our human frailties. So why do we expect them to stop now?

In the digital era, we have ushered in a new term, 'social engineering', to describe the act of being duped into providing information or handing over money to these fraudsters via whatever means they deem appropriate. From phishing (email) to vishing (telephone calls), these fraudsters will try to convince us to hand over money or information under the pretext that they are from some official or trusted entity. From the tax office to law enforcement, anyone can be impersonated. No one is exempt, and everyone is a target. These fraudsters will manipulate our moods and emotions to extract from us what they want.

Cyber criminals will exploit our greed by emailing us with offers of great riches or huge discounts on goods that are 'just too good to be true'. With every new release of games consoles and mobile devices, there is a deluge of phishing emails offering 50% discounts or early access to these 'must have' items, as they implore us to "buy now or miss out!".

There are also 'foreign princes' who have millions that just need to be transferred out of their country, and promises of early entry into a new cryptocurrency market.

Criminals will exploit our vanity by offering weight loss or hair replacement treatments, and they will take advantage of our fears by offering health tablets that can cure everything from cancer to COVID-19. On occasion, I have been asked if these people have morals. I have no answer to this except to say that they are ruthless, skilled, highly motivated – and don't care. Perhaps that's a long way of saying 'No', I don't believe they have morals, or at least not the same ones you and I have. But again, this is a complex matter as we're dealing with human motivations, feelings and situations. In many developing countries where the need to feed a family can be satisfied by working at a call centre that operates as a front to cyber crime, poverty and self-preservation are the motives behind this crime. Criminals will often 'victim blame', where they externalise their actions and say things like *"Well if they had invested in better security..."*, and *"They shouldn't have been so stupid to fall for such an obvious con."*. This goes some way to answer the question, *"How do these people sleep at night?"* Criminals also quite often see their crimes as victimless, as they often assert that ultimately banks will pay out, and people can claim on their insurance. Of course, this isn't always the case and is just an easy way for them to disassociate themselves from the harm they cause.

Fear is perhaps the most common and effective emotion that cyber criminals use, as it's a great motivator and can easily be invoked in any of us, whether it's an email from an irate supplier who hasn't been paid, the police threatening a speeding fine, or the tax office chasing for tax return documentation.

17: The clever general

As Sun Tzu observes, the clever general will avoid us when our spirits are keen but will attack when we're sluggish and tired. Consider that 'conveyance fraud' is also known as 'Friday fraud' because cyber criminals take advantage of a busy day for the legal sector, where large funds transfer hurriedly before the weekend. They take advantage of the fact that people are 'sluggish' and less attentive because they are tired, under pressure, and in a hurry to start their weekend.

During the COVID-19 pandemic, we have all suffered from FUD, but we are also working longer hours as our work start and end times become blurred. We have become increasingly tired and anxious, and cyber criminals know this and use this against us. We need to recognise that our teams are also tired and anxious and can become victims. This is why it's important to understand and study the moods of the people we seek to serve, to prevent criminals taking advantage. The questions I will leave you with are:

1. How are you going to change your approach to cyber security to maximise the moods of those around you?
2. How do you think cyber criminals will use our moods to exploit those you seek to serve and protect?

"Disciplined and calm, to await the appearance of disorder and hubbub amongst the enemy - this is the art of retaining self-possession."

Sun Tzu

CHAPTER 18: DISCIPLINED AND CALM

Over a millennium, our minds and bodies evolved to react to the life-threatening situations we found ourselves in. This fight-or-flight response is an automatic physiological reaction to an event perceived as stressful, dangerous or frightening and it was highly effective when dangerous beasts roamed around our neighbourhood. The perception of threat activates the sympathetic nervous system and triggers an acute stress response that prepares the body for battle or to head with haste for the nearest place of safety.

Our neanderthal ancestors would have had such a response when faced with a sabre-toothed tiger. Although the risks we face today aren't quite so dramatic, our physiology doesn't know this. When faced with a stressful or frightening situation, we are still prone to the same reactions! From the stress we feel when stepping out on stage in front of a live audience to that sinking feeling we get when we learn we've suffered a cyber attack – the fight, flee or freeze response is just as real and alive today as it ever was.

People often talk about that 'sinking feeling' or feeling 'sick to the stomach' in response to a stressful or significantly challenging situation. They talk about feeling as if time has slowed as their heart rates quicken. Some talk about being 'gripped by fear', and 'paralysed' and incapable of making rational decisions.

What is happening, in reality, is that in the face of this perceived (or actual) crisis situation, our neanderthal brain kicks in, and we are suddenly back fighting for our lives. This can be useful in real life-threatening conditions, but can be debilitating in day-to-day activities. The amygdala is part of the brain that coordinates responses to what's going on around you, especially those events that trigger an emotional response – such as fear. When you touch, see, hear, taste or experience something, this information is first relayed to the thalamus. The thalamus then passes this information to your neocortex (often referred to as the 'thinking brain') then to the amygdala (the 'emotional brain'), which produces the most appropriate emotional response (disgust, shock, fear, pain, arousal, etc.). But when faced with a threatening situation, the thalamus relays the information to BOTH the amygdala and the neocortex at the same time. If the amygdala senses danger, it will overrule the neocortex, and the response will be emotional. This all happens in a nano-second, as our bodies flood with the hormones epinephrine (aka adrenaline) and cortisol.

When faced with a cyber attack or the repercussions of an attack, it is easy to imagine how our amygdala can be hijacked, and we would find ourselves in the 'fight, flight or freeze' vortex. It is these feelings that Sun Tzu states that we must combat to ensure we retain self-possession. But how do we remain disciplined and calm in these situations?

The survival arc

In her 2008 disaster survival book *The Unthinkable*, Amanda Ripley identifies the common response patterns of people in disaster or threatening situations and states that they are based on three phases: denial, deliberation and decision. She states that these make up the 'survival arc', and where the bell curve is low and long, the more likely for crisis and disaster. But the quicker we can move from denial to decision (or decisive action), the more likely we will retain control and survive the event we're facing. Although her book talks about everything from facing a gunman to surviving an air traffic accident, I believe this survival arc is also relevant to the cyber security professional.

Denial

It's likely that you've experienced this phase of the arc in your life when faced with a significant event or potential calamity. For example, have you ever been in a place with other people when a fire alarm goes off? What was your reaction, and theirs? Did everyone immediately run to the exits? Did you? Probably not. Sat at your desk, chances are you looked up and around at what they were doing. Just like a group of curious meerkats, others would look back at you as if surveying the level of risk around you, and even though you probably had a creeping sense of dread, you ignored it and returned to what you were doing.

This isn't something that relates to some unseen calamity, like an alarm. During the 9/11 attack, survivors reported that some people on the lower floors of the World Trade Center remained at their desks, finishing calls or emails or chatting calmly to colleagues about what was happening. It was reported that they waited an average of five minutes before taking action. It may seem strange to consider, but generally speaking, there was no mass panic when the evacuation did begin. It wasn't like the movies with people running and screaming. Instead, many people calmly marched out of their offices, down the stairwells, taking verbal and non-verbal cues from those around them.

This phase of the survival arc can be put down to the cognitive bias known as the 'normalcy bias'. This cognitive bias leads people to minimise or disbelieve the threats or threat warnings around us. Those people in the twin towers heard the rumble of the plane impacting the building and felt it shake, yet they still took five minutes to make a decision.

If you think this is a new phenomenon, think again. Mount Vesuvius erupted in 79 AD, burying the city of Pompeii, killing an estimated 2,000 of the 16,000 inhabitants.

This shows that 14,000 did evacuate and escape, but the eruption didn't start out especially dangerous in a manner that made people want to flee right away. Many sheltered first, perhaps preferring to imagine it wasn't going to get any worse. But as the hours passed and the eruption increased in intensity people eventually considered evacuating. For some it was too late.

Deliberation

As the events unfolded on 9/11, people paused to clear and pack away their things or returned to their desks to collect laptops and other personal belongings. In 79 AD, people stood and watched for hours as Vesuvius erupted and spewed lava down towards the city of Pompei. People stood watching what was happening, deliberating and discussing what action they should take. The normalcy bias was operating at full force here, but there is also another influence at play here: social influence. It may sound surprising, but people fail to act because they don't wish to appear foolish.

Several experiments have taken place to test the idea of social influence, but possibly the most famous is the 1969 'Smoke Study'. In the study, volunteers were left in a waiting room to fill out a questionnaire before the experiment had begun. However, unknown to them, the experiment was already in full flow. As they completed the form, smoke pumped through a vent. When the volunteer was alone, they looked around briefly, then returned to the questionnaire, but as the room filled with smoke, they took action within 30 to 60 seconds. This happened approximately 75% of the time.

Next, participants sat in the room with two other participants who were equally unaware that the experiment had begun. This resulted in them reporting smoke 38% of the time and took considerably longer to take action, as they sat looking at each other to see who would take action first. In the final experiment, a volunteer was accompanied by two others who were aware of what was going on and part of the team conducting the experiment. The two people pretended not to notice the smoke, which resulted in the volunteer sitting in the room for considerably longer than earlier participants. Only 10% of them reported the smoke to someone.

This experiment has been repeated many times, with varying groups, but the basic premise is always the same, culminating with a volunteer sat among active participants. In every case, as the alarm sounded, smoke filled the room, the volunteers waited an average of seven minutes before taking action, seemingly unable to act. Why? Because they didn't want to be the first person to react in a room full of strangers. This social influence is known more commonly as the 'bystander effect', and various studies have taken place to prove that this is a very real and very present risk for us all.[19]

Now imagine how much stronger the impact of social influencing is on those people who lead our businesses. They know that their standing in the (business) community could be at risk if they act too quickly or in a way that could be deemed to be overreacting. The normalcy bias and social

---

[19] *www.redcross.org.uk/stories/health-and-social-care/first-aid/what-is-the-bystander-effect*.

influencing psychological tricks (traps?) have a lot to answer for, but recognising that they are there and we can all suffer from them should help us when faced with a significant event in our lives. One way to combat these traps is to conduct regular exercises so that major events become 'normal', and therefore if faced with something similar in the future, we are less likely to downplay the impact of the event. This is why crisis management exercises are so important and why I tell people to test their plans and exercise their teams. Building familiarity with different scenarios is essential. Building understanding with others in the team also helps combat the risk that social influence will lead to denial or deliberation.

Decisive action

It should be clear by now that the quicker we can move from denial and deliberation to decisive action, the greater the chance we'll survive. Helping those around us to move through this arc is at the heart of crisis and business continuity exercises. There is no way of knowing what the future holds, and we know we can't stop these calamities from occurring, but as I often say to people, *"Don't be led by the crisis. You must lead it!"*

This is the essence of a disciplined and calm response to a significant event. If you can remain calm and retain self-possession, you'll embody what Sun Tzu is asking of us. Or, to paraphrase Rudyard Kipling;

"If you can keep your head when all about you are losing theirs, you'll be a Man, my son."

"There are five dangerous faults which may affect a general..."

Sun Tzu

CHAPTER 19: FIVE DANGEROUS FAULTS

Leading an organisation is never a simple task, and leading in cyber security is especially difficult. But leadership is critical if cyber security and data protection practices are to be successful. Clause 5.1 of ISO 27001 is 'Leadership', so you will need to evidence this if you implement this standard successfully. The keyword here is *evidence*. But how do you evidence something which is an ethereal topic? Ask five people what leadership is, and you'll get five different answers. So here are a couple of questions for you:

- What is leadership?
- Think of four leaders you know of (from history or your own life) – what traits do these leaders have? Are they perfect examples of humanity, or are there dangerous faults that we need to be aware of?

Sun Tzu tells us that the following faults may affect leaders, so we should be guarded against them:

1. **Recklessness**, which leads to destruction.
2. **Cowardice**, which leads to capture.
3. **A hasty temper**, which can be provoked by insults.
4. **A delicacy of honour** which is sensitive to shame.
5. **Over-solicitude for his men**, which exposes him to worry and trouble.

Are any of the leaders you thought of flawed by these? Let's take a look.

Recklessness, leading to destruction

The definition of reckless is to be *"heedless of danger or the consequences of one's actions; rash or impetuous"*. Therefore, good leaders are thoughtful, cautious, responsible, and consider the needs and concerns of everyone under their command and control. Good leaders do not act recklessly and with haste. Taking time to consider the risks (and opportunities) before the event and view all available options once the enemy is engaged is vital if you're to be successful in any endeavour, especially in times of crisis. Reckless leaders tend to be the ones who believe that they are the only person that has all the answers and knows the perfect solution. In 'peace times' (aka business as usual (BAU)), acting recklessly can be dangerous, but it can be destructive in times of stress and crisis. During these times of increased stress, leaders need to step back and listen to their generals and team more intently.

To put it bluntly; crisis management teams need to be led by someone who isn't listening to their ego or struggling to fight their neanderthal brain. By working with the team, leaders are more likely to make rational and informed decisions, which is all we can really ask of our leaders. They are the ones who make the difficult decisions, but only after they have been given all available facts.

Now, you may be thinking that this is fine during times of BAU, but in times of crisis, this isn't possible. But I would respectfully disagree. I believe it's *more* important during times of crisis to gather what information we can about what has happened or happening and then step back, pause, consult with our team and consider our next step before taking action. Acting recklessly at this stage can simply lead to more trouble or create a larger problem to deal with, and you'll either be pouring oil on troubled waters or fanning the flames.

Cowardice, which leads to capture

In a business context, I believe cowardice is evidence of the inability to make a decision or willingness to listen to those around you. It may be linked to the normalcy bias we discussed earlier, but generally speaking, I believe it is the inability to make a decision when in the midst of combat for fear that it will lead to failure (i.e. capture) and, therefore, a fall from grace, and status. We all must understand that a leader doesn't have all the answers. They make decisions based on all the available information presented to them. Consider for a moment the role of the head of state, such as the President of the United States. They can't be expected to know and do everything. They have extremely complex decisions to make, but their role is to make these decisions based on all available information. President Barack Obama shared his approach to making decisions in a blog post on the platform Medium. In this frank discussion on making decisions, he made the following statement:

> *"When you have a tough, almost unsolvable decision to make, you don't just want people to tell you what you want to hear."*

You can read the complete piece here:

https://barackobama.medium.com/how-i-approach-the-toughest-decisions-dc1b165cdf2d.

It takes courage to listen to those around you, especially when they go against your own thoughts or opinions, and when that decision could reflect negatively on you. But this is 'ego' taking control. And failure to take action because of fear of what might happen to you could ultimately lead to defeat.

A hasty temper, which can be provoked by insults

To quote an Internet meme, "Lions do not turn around when a dog barks". If they have acted in the best interests of those they look to lead and serve, leaders shouldn't be quick to anger when the world seems against them. Anger is an emotion that is deep-rooted in many of us and can lead us to act recklessly, thereby placing our organisations and us at risk. When someone acts in haste, they do not weigh up all the options thoroughly and certainly wouldn't be aware of all the stacked odds for or against them.

Again, Barack Obama's blog post gives us insight into his approach to making tough decisions. He spends time alone so he can think through the issues and problems he is faced with before making the difficult decisions. He is not swayed by popular opinion (although I am sure it is a consideration). This is important. Making decisions based on what others say is once again pandering to the ego. Basing decisions on emotion such as anger is likely to result in ruin as all the available options are not going to be fully considered.

Taking a few moments to consider the appropriate actions is advisable when faced with difficult decisions, and in times of crisis, it becomes increasingly important – especially when the 'Twittersphere' may be screaming insults at you.

A delicacy of honour which is sensitive to shame

Much of what we do is so public that it's easy to worry about what others think, to the point that it is debilitating. As social media ignites at the actions and inactions we take, successful leaders must be willing to do what is unpopular. Being overly cautious about public opinion might lead to a reluctance to act because of a fear of shame, ridicule or embarrassment. I've seen this in action as crisis looms, and leaders are unable or unwilling to take action for fear of what others might think of them. I've also seen this play out in boardrooms where CISOs refuse to discuss the latest risks or incident reports for fear of the personal impact on their standing in the C-suite and their reputation. The results of penetration tests are diluted so that they don't lead to admonishment, blame and shame. Putting the greater good of the organisation or those you seek to serve first is often tricky but is an essential quality of any good leader.

Over-solicitude for his men

A leader cannot know everything, and they must collect all available data and information from their team. A leader must care about those they lead, but being overly anxious and protective can lead us to become hesitant before making a difficult decision. This is closely linked to the danger of having a delicacy of honour. The over-solicitous leader is unable to make a decision because they care too much about what people think about them. Being solicitous means you would rather lose (i.e. suffer defeat at the hands of an external attacker) than lose face with those you lead.

We should keep the words of Barack Obama in mind:

"Our choices reflect and determine who we are."

But these words shouldn't shackle us and prevent us from making decisions. When faced with difficult decisions, either in times of peace or crisis, we need to remove ourselves from the equation and ask what decisions we would make if there was no risk of impact on us, personally. Therefore, when considering this area, ask yourself how much ego plays a part in your decision-making process and how much ego is in play in your crisis management team.

As Sun Tzu observes:

> *"These are the five besetting sins of a general, ruinous to the conduct of war. When an army is overthrown and its leader slain, the cause will surely be found among these five dangerous faults. Let them be a subject of meditation."*

I believe the cause will ultimately boil down to one of ego. That's something worth meditating on, too.

"If soldiers are punished before they have grown attached to you, they will not prove submissive; and, unless submissive, then will be practically useless.

If, when the soldiers have become attached to you, punishments are not enforced, they will still be unless."

Sun Tzu

CHAPTER 20: SOLDIERS

Although it is not our aim to have a submissive workforce, it is essential that everyone entering your organisation is fully aware of the policies and procedures in place and the impact of breaching them. This means *everybody* in your organisation, irrespective of role and position. All too often, we hear how rank-and-file employees are expected to complete induction training, yet directors and senior leaders in a business aren't. The head of the organisation (perhaps the business owner) is often at fault here. If they themselves display no interest in the policies and processes that govern their business, then why should anyone else?

We have already discussed the importance of education and awareness around the risks associated with cyber security and data protection, such as phishing and ransomware. But we should also clearly explain people's roles and responsibilities in association with these topics. At every level, our teams need to understand what is expected of them and how they must act to ensure they are operating safely and securely. This is often outlined in policies, such as the 'acceptable use policy', where we make clear what the organisation deems appropriate (i.e. acceptable) behaviour when using organisational assets. These assets often include acceptable use of data, the Internet, social media, email and devices.

It's vitally important that this information is provided when the team member joins the organisation so they understand the impact their actions (or inaction) can have on them and your organisation. This is what Sun Tzu refers to when he talks of soldiers being 'attached to you'. Suppose we don't communicate effectively from the outset. In that case, soldiers will 'still be useless', but we must ensure we share policies and reassert them periodically (as they become more familiar with us). When someone first starts at an organisation, there is a lot of information to take on board; therefore, their ability to retain information related to topics like cyber security, data protection, and what is and is not acceptable is likely to be reduced. One method to combat this is to leave this training until the end of induction and insist on committing to (at least) an annual review and revision.

At this point, I will reiterate the importance of ensuring policies are consistently applied at all levels of the organisation. Otherwise, there will be discord among the employees you look to lead. Sun Tzu makes the point expertly:

> *"If in training soldiers commands are habitually enforced, the army will be well-disciplined; if not, its discipline will be bad."*

I have seen organisations fail in their attempts to implement cyber security due to the fact that senior leaders don't think the policies and procedures apply to them. Arrogance, ignorance or complacency have led them to believe that they are above such things and that policies and procedures only apply to lower positions. We need to ensure everyone in the organisation understands how policies apply to them and their role. They need to understand that policies provide a clear vision of what the organisation is looking to achieve and ensure reputation and brand protection. Policies and procedures provide the confidence that every leader needs, and this benefits everyone.

"If a general shows confidence in his men but always insists on his orders being obeyed, the gain will be mutual."

At first glance, it may look as though Sun Tzu had a low opinion of soldiers, but this is not true. He believed in the importance of respect, and ensuring everyone understands their role is one sign of respect. Sun Tzu went on to talk about soldiers more compassionately when he said the following:

"Regard your soldiers as your children, and they will follow you into the deepest valleys; look upon them as your own beloved sons, and they will stand by you even unto death."

I feel this is something that organisations get wrong all the time. They talk about how the 'customer is king', and the 'customer comes first', but this isn't true at all.

Your people come first.

Your people are king.

Your people should be treated as 'your own beloved sons'.

To put it bluntly, you won't have happy customers for very long if your people are unhappy and feeling resentful of you or the leadership team. Why would someone be willing to go that extra mile, or even that extra inch, when they are not valued by the people who lead them? Some might say it's because that's what they're paid for, but this is a short-sighted view. Competitors will be happy to pay your teams too, so what's stopping them from leaving? Other opportunities will present themselves, so what's stopping them from taking these opportunities? There are always opportunities for people to leave a poorly run organisation. There is an oft-quoted statement that *"People don't leave bad jobs, they leave bad bosses"*. I don't know who said this, but it's accurate. If attrition is bad within an organisation, the people team should take a close look at the leadership team to understand what is wrong there rather than simply calculating numbers and increasing salaries and 'benefits'. The benefit of working for an organisation is that you feel as though you are part of something meaningful and that you are respected and loved (yes, loved) by those around you.

Sun Tzu urges us to have submissive soldiers who we treat as our beloved sons. There is a complexity here that requires careful consideration and meditation. But ultimately, I believe it's about showing respect to our teams by explaining to them what we expect of them so that they follow our guidance and controls (submissive), while also encouraging them and supporting them as we would our own children.

"Hostile armies may face each other for years, striving for the victory which is decided in a single day.

This being so, to remain in ignorance of the enemy's condition simply because one grudges the outlay of a hundred ounces of silver in honours and emoluments is the height of inhumanity."

Sun Tzu

CHAPTER 21: STRIVING FOR VICTORY

Protecting an organisation from cyber attack or breaches is hard work. To repeat the IRA's chilling message to Margaret Thatcher, a central edict of cyber criminals is: *"Today we were unlucky, but remember we only have to be lucky once. You will have to be lucky always."* You may be working hard for months and years to implement technologies, plans and processes that are never needed. The awful truth is, you'll never know if you've done enough until they're tested, and as we all know, there is no 100% guarantee that they will work. It has already been said that we are in the midst of a global 'arms race' where the enemy is working hard to gain access to our systems and data.

While you are sleeping, those looking to do us harm are automating their processes and indiscriminately carrying out their attacks against unsuspecting and possibly complacent targets. Complacency is a problem for us because it is easy for this feeling to set in, especially when nothing happens. Leaders in an organisation can become complacent about existing risks and ignorant of new ones. In times where money and resources are stretched, I have seen the security team budget slashed as the C-suite begrudges spending on defences that they perceive to be unrequired. I believe this has led to the increase in cyber insurance, which is again giving the C-suite a false sense of security, that should something happen, they will be able to make a claim. It's a dangerous assumption, as cyber insurance products are still in their infancy and are still subject to exemptions. Additionally, it's worth knowing that cyber criminals are targeting insurance companies to discover who has insurance so that they can target those organisations (as they are potentially more likely to pay ransom demands).

As security professionals, a large part of our role is to ensure that we are not blighted by either complacency or ignorance. We know our leaders can suffer from these if left to their own devices. A mechanism to reduce the risk of complacency is to clearly define the benefits of implementing a robust cyber security and data protection compliance programme. Focusing merely on the adverse effects of an attack will only get you so far, and while the strategy is excellent during times of war, it is a low motivator during times of relative and perceived peace. Although we know that an attack can come at any time, the perception in the C-suite is that nothing has happened, and therefore doesn't require constant attention. This is the exact ignorance that Sun Tzu speaks of. We need a strategy to deal with it, and that strategy is to highlight the benefits of implementing a cyber security and data protection programme. We discussed this earlier by highlighting the needs of each of the people sitting around the C-suite, but it's worth returning to these to remind ourselves of some of the benefits of getting our compliance programme right.

These benefits include:

- Increased trust with suppliers and customers;
- Increase in brand value;
- Reduction of incidents and events (e.g. breaches, lost laptops, etc.);
- Better management of information assets;
- Reduced costs and company spend;
- Reduction in information-related risks;
- Increased efficiency and productivity (ensuring the right

information is available at the right time to only the right people);

- Understanding your legal and other requirements – then managing them;
- Improving and protecting your reputation – not only the legal requirements but also better managing and reducing near-misses and incidents;
- Improved organisational resilience; and
- Increase in staff morale (no one likes working at a company that has lots of breaches!).

It may be challenging, but we must think in terms of the business and benefits, rather than security professionals and protection. For example, rather than thinking about 'brand protection' (which we often do), we should think in terms of increased brand value. Increased brand value is more likely to excite everyone in the C-suite, get them interested, and garner more support.

Setting clearly defined measures and metrics that allow us to demonstrate these positive objectives will ensure we obtain and maintain continual support for what we are there to do, preparing for the battle yet to come.

"He who knows these things, and in fighting puts his knowledge into practice, will win his battles.

He who knows them not, nor practises them, will surely be defeated."

Sun Tzu

CHAPTER 22: CONCLUSION

> ***"To know and not do, is not to know."***
>
> Stephen R. Covey (author, coach and businessman)

If you have reached this point, then congratulations – you have begun to explore the idea of becoming an artist and looking at this cyber security profession from a different perspective.

However, the hard work starts now. As Stephen R. Covey observed, there's no point in knowing something if you're not going to act on it. The hardest part is combating our fears of standing out from the crowd and being seen differently, but you were born to stand out – not blend in! I am a fully committed business romantic; I love what I do, and I have no hesitation in writing those words or telling people. I'm passionate and excited about what we do and about the future. Isn't that a better way to talk about what we do than saying it's a bit 'dull' or worse … boring?

The world needs more artists. We need more people who are in love with what they do and have a fire inside them and who are willing to play with the idea that they can make a difference – because they can. Let your inner child go free, learn to play, create and do something truly magnificent! Why can't a policy be equal to the sonnets of William Shakespeare? Why can't a PowerPoint presentation bristle with the energy of a Picasso painting? I believe they can, and if you think they can, then you're halfway there. To create something beautiful and share it with the world is the noblest of things.

22: Conclusion

Although most of this book focuses on the works of Sun Tzu, its principal aim is to encourage you to see the world differently, through the eyes of an artist. There are many other quotes and passages within *The Art of War*. I encourage you to read it. Perhaps you will find other quotes you feel I should have included – I'd love to know which passages resonate with you and why. Perhaps you could expand on this book, and your input can make it into the next edition. I think it takes great imagination to think deeply about a topic and see it differently from everyone else. That's why there is no right or wrong approach to this art.

Steve Jobs did this magnificently as he gazed into the future. He saw a world where people are capable of doing great things with the technology he reimagined. He saw the future in terms of people who are brave enough to challenge the norm and create something special. In one of the many famous quotes attributed to Jobs, he encapsulates what it is to be an artist:

"Here's to the crazy ones, the misfits, the rebels, the troublemakers, the round pegs in the square holes. The ones who see things differently - they're not fond of rules, and they have no respect for the status quo. You can quote them, disagree with them, glorify or vilify them, but the only thing you can't do is ignore them because they change things. They push the human race forward, and while some may see them as the crazy ones, we see genius because the people who are crazy enough to think that they can change the world are the ones who do."

I love this quote and have used it many times as inspiration in my career. I am happy to think that I am in this group of 'misfits', and I hope you are too because we have the opportunity to do AMAZING things!

We shouldn't pass up on this opportunity.

I would like to leave you with one of my all-time favourite quotes, from artist and author Gordon MacKenzie, who illustrates the central theme of this book perfectly:

> *"How many artists are there in the room? Would you please raise your hands?*
>
> *First Grade: En masse, the children leapt from their seats, arms waving.*
> *Every child was an artist.*
>
> *Second Grade: About half the kids raised their hands, shoulder high, but no higher.*
> *The hands were still.*
>
> *Third Grade: At best, ten kids out of thirty would raise a hand tentatively, self-consciously.*
>
> *By the time I reached Sixth Grade, no more than one or two kids raised their hands, and then ever so slightly, betraying a fear of being identified by the group as a 'closet artist'.*
>
> *The point is: Every school I visited was participating in the systematic suppression of creative genius."*

I hope these words will spur you to action. We are all artists. You are an artist. I want you to rekindle your inner artist and start to think and see yourselves differently. It's not just important as we move towards an increasingly technologically led world, it's vital.

You need this.

We need this.

The world needs this.

There is an artist hidden inside you. Set them free.

You should meditate on this.

CHAPTER 23: REQUIRED READING

For more information on the ideas and concepts mentioned in this book, take a look at the following titles. This isn't the normal list of 'reading' you'd find in cyber security books. That's because this is no ordinary cyber security book. In fact, there is only one book in the list that directly relates to information security.

Instead, I chose books that inspired me, helped shape my view of the world and the contents of these pages. I have learned something important from each, either about cyber security or about my approach to the topic. They can help you too.

All the publications are also available as audiobooks, so there's really no excuse not to explore them!

Enjoy.

All Marketers Are Liars – Seth Godin

Art & Fear – David Bayles, Ted Orland

Atlas of the Heart – Brené Brown

Atomic Habits – James Clear

Be Water, My Friend – Shannon Lee

Black Box Thinking – Matthew Syed

Brainfluence – Roger Dooley

Braving the Wilderness – Brené Brown

Contagious – Jonah Berger

Conversational Intelligence – Judith E. Glaser

Creativity, Inc. – Ed Catmull

Dare to Lead – Brené Brown

Enchantment – Guy Kawaskai

Fire Them Up! – Carmine Gallo

Five Stars – Carmine Gallo

Good to Great – Jim Collins

Happy Sexy Millionaire – Steven Bartlett

High Performance – Jake Humphrey, Damian Hughes

How to Win Friends and Influence People – Dale Carnegie

Key Person of Influence – Daniel Priestley

Limitless – Jim Kwik

Man's Search for Meaning – Victor E. Frankl

Opportunity – Rob Moore

Oversubscribed – Daniel Priestley

Real Influence – John Ullmen, Mark Goulston

Rebel Ideas – Matthew Syed

Rethink Social Media – Paul O'Mahony

Rising Strong – Brené Brown

Start Now. Get Perfect Later. – Rob Moore

23: Required reading

Start with Why – Simon Sinek

Stolen Focus – Johann Hari

Switch – Chip Heath, Dan Heath

The 7 Habits of Highly Effective People – Stephen R. Covey

The Art of Creative Thinking – Rod Judkins

The Art of War – Sun Tzu

The Choice – Edith Eger

The E-Myth Revisited – Michael E. Gerber

The Hard Thing About Hard Things – Ben Horowitz

The Icarus Deception – Seth Godin

The Leader Who Had No Title – Robin Sharma

The Little Big Things – Tom Peters

The Magic of Thinking Big – David Schwartz

The Monk Who Sold His Ferrari – Robin Sharma

The One Thing – Gary Keller, Jay Papasan

The Storyteller's Secret – Carmine Gallo

The Speed of Trust – Stephen M.R. Covey

The Subtle Art of Not Giving a F*ck – Mark Manson

This is Marketing – Seth Godin

Tiny Beautiful Things – Cheryl Strayed

Transformational Security Awareness – Perry Carpenter

23: Required reading

Tribe of Mentors – Tim Ferriss

Tribes – Seth Godin

Unscripted – MJ DeMarco

Wabi Sabi – Beth Kempton

Yes! 50 Secrets from the Science of Persuasion – Dr Noah Goldstein, Steve Martin, Dr Robert Cialdini

FURTHER READING

IT Governance Publishing (ITGP) is the world's leading publisher for governance and compliance. Our industry-leading pocket guides, books, training resources and toolkits are written by real-world practitioners and thought leaders. They are used globally by audiences of all levels, from students to C-suite executives.

Our high-quality publications cover all IT governance, risk and compliance frameworks and are available in a range of formats. This ensures our customers can access the information they need in the way they need it.

Our other publications about cyber security include:

- *Digital Earth – Cyber threats, privacy and ethics in an age of paranoia* by Sarah Katz,
  www.itgovernancepublishing.co.uk/product/digital-earth
- *The Cyber Security Handbook – Prepare for, respond to and recover from cyber attacks with the IT Governance Cyber Resilience Framework (CRF)* by Alan Calder,
  www.itgovernancepublishing.co.uk/product/the-cyber-security-handbook-prepare-for-respond-to-and-recover-from-cyber-attacks
- *The Ransomware Threat Landscape – Prepare for, recognise and survive ransomware attacks* by Alan Calder,

www.itgovernancepublishing.co.uk/product/the-ransomware-threat-landscape

For more information on ITGP and branded publishing services, and to view our full list of publications, visit *www.itgovernancepublishing.co.uk*.

To receive regular updates from ITGP, including information on new publications in your area(s) of interest, sign up for our newsletter at *www.itgovernancepublishing.co.uk/topic/newsletter*.

Branded publishing

Through our branded publishing service, you can customise ITGP publications with your company's branding.

Find out more at:

www.itgovernancepublishing.co.uk/topic/branded-publishing-services.

Related services

ITGP is part of GRC International Group, which offers a comprehensive range of complementary products and services to help organisations meet their objectives.

For a full range of resources on cyber security visit *www.itgovernance.co.uk/what-is-cybersecurity*.

Training services

The IT Governance training programme is built on our extensive practical experience designing and implementing management systems based on ISO standards, best practice and regulations.

Our courses help attendees develop practical skills and comply with contractual and regulatory requirements. They also support career development via recognised qualifications.

Learn more about our training courses in cyber security and view the full course catalogue at *www.itgovernance.co.uk/training*.

Professional services and consultancy

We are a leading global consultancy of IT governance, risk management and compliance solutions. We advise businesses around the world on their most critical issues and present cost-saving and risk-reducing solutions based on international best practice and frameworks.

We offer a wide range of delivery methods to suit all budgets, timescales and preferred project approaches.

Find out how our consultancy services can help your organisation at *www.itgovernance.co.uk/consulting*.

Industry news

Want to stay up to date with the latest developments and resources in the IT governance and compliance market? Subscribe to our Weekly Round-up newsletter and we will send you mobile-friendly emails with fresh news and features about your preferred areas of interest, as well as unmissable offers and free resources to help you successfully start your projects. *www.itgovernance.co.uk/weekly-round-up*.

EU for product safety is Stephen Evans, The Mill Enterprise Hub, Stagreenan, Drogheda, Co. Louth, A92 CD3D, Ireland. (servicecentre@itgovernance.eu)